Pacific Standard Time
New & Selected Poems

Kevin Opstedal

Pacific Standard Time: New & Selected Poems
Copyright © Kevin Opstedal, 2016

ISBN 978-1-937027-80-3

First Edition, First Printing 2016

Ugly Duckling Presse
The Old American Can Factory
232 Third Street, E-303
Brooklyn, NY 11215
uglyducklingpresse.org

Distributed to the trade by Small Press Distribution
www.spdbooks.org

Design by K Jaeger and Don't Look Now!
Typeset in Jenson and Verlag by K Jaeger
Cover photograph "Bolinas 2003" by Pamela Dewey © 2016

Printed and bound by McNaughton & Gunn, Saline, MI
Covers printed by Prestige Printing, Brooklyn, NY

Support for this publication was provided
by a generous grant from the
National Endowment for the Arts

ART WORKS.

Pacific Standard Time
New & Selected Poems

Kevin Opstedal

Edited by Noel Black
and Julien Poirier

Ugly Duckling Presse
Brooklyn, NY
2016

Table of Contents

III

Bansai Palm Trees, or:
Pre-Apocalyptic Romanticism and the
Psychogeographic California Landscape
Poetry of Kevin Opstedal

I'm holding in my hands something close to the collected poems of Kevin Opstedal. Not this book you're reading now, but the 6 or 7 pounds of staple-bound chapbooks and small-run perfect-bound collections that have arrived in my mailbox over the past 20 years. They always came in little hardboard manila mailers with a white slip of paper on which he'd have neatly scrawled a note in an all-caps script worn smooth like sea glass.

NOEL,

HEREIN PLEASE FIND
THE SOUND OF ONE
LEAD BALLOON POPPING
ABOVE ZUMA BEACH

KEVIN, OCT. 1, '09

The titles:

Minus Tide
Heavy Water
Radio Beach
Sunset Revisited
Variable High Cloudiness
Coastal Disturbance (Bikini Machine)
Maybe Ocean Street
Rare Surf, Vol. 2: New & Used Poems
The Poetikal Works of Dude the Obscure
Beach Blanket Massacre
The Deep End
Sand in the Vaseline
California Redemption Value

And on.

Some (many) were self-published on presses he'd invented for the publication of that particular book, or until he got bored with the name:

> Surf Zombie
> Smog Eyes
> Plywood Press
> Blue Press
> Pale Music Press
> Pelican Press

On the covers:

Palm trees, ocean horizons, a baja bug, more horizons, more palm trees, a monkey on surfboard, a monkey carrying a surf board, the Silver Surfer, waves, beach. On the cover of *Coastal Disturbance (Bikini Machine)* there's a photo of Kevin taken by his partner, the photographer Pamela Dewey. He's standing in front of a heavily graffitied palm tree at Venice Beach where he grew up. His uniform: a gray, short-sleeved T-shirt over white, long-sleeved t-shirt, hands stuffed into his jean pockets, Ray-Ban cat-eyes perched on his nose beneath his waves of Norwegian red hair: Dude, the Obscure.

For me and many others who orbited New College of California in San Francisco in the late 1990s, Kevin's *Gas Magazine* was a kind of wormhole to the last days of the New York School via Bolinas, Los Angeles and back to the San Francisco scene at the time. Eileen Myles, Bernadette Mayer, Ted Berrigan, Ron Padgett, Charles Bukowski, Joanne Kyger, Alice Notley, Hoa Nguyen, Harry Mathews—household names in contemporary poetry now—were regulars in the table of contents. I'd never have heard of most of them in those pre-internet days but for Gas.

It would be easy, perhaps, to talk about the general aesthetic/ philosophical opposition to L=A=N=G=U=A=G=E that

Gas represented at the time. But for most of us it was more like indifference—a distaste for the ideology, theory, and jobs in favor of wit, style, and jokes. *Gas* was the lifeblood for this vein of sexier, admittedly white-trash American poetry that was playing out there on the West coast in the wake of *The New American Poetry/Post-Modern American Poetry*. None of us saw the internet coming to the degree that it did even as it rose up around us there in the Bay Area, nor did we particularly care. And we certainly didn't see the rise of the MFA programs and their influence on small-press publishing that was already on its way. What we'd picked up, and took away, was the New York School/Black Mountain/Berkeley-Spicer aesthetics (and its baggage, of course), to some extent. But to a greater extent it was the means of production: stolen photocopies; staples; linoleum-block-cut covers run on Vandercook presses or silk-screened at the Mission Cultural Center; late-night, Ritalin-fueled staple-n-stuff mailing parties. It was a way of being social at a time when we didn't fully realize the bohemian/punk life we'd romanticized had died during the Reagan years and would soon rise from the grave as Facebook. I don't think I'm overstating it when I say that none of us thought poetry would get us anywhere, or that it should, or that it could. The idea that you'd write the kind of poetry we wanted to write and get a job teaching was laughable, even at a place like New College or Naropa (more hippie than hip in those days). But, naively or not, we still believed in poetry as a means to its own end.

Kevin Opstedal was our champion—a working-class poet-publisher anti-saint who had a shit maintenance job in a corporate office park in Silicon Valley and lived for "The Poems." He snuck photocopies from the machines at night, or outsourced larger jobs to some friends known only as "The Tongans." There was nothing greater than getting a freshly stapled magazine or chapbook in the mail from Kevin. So why would you aspire to do anything more or less than that? If the now-canonized "Mission School" artists of the time—Margaret Kilgallen, Barry McGee, Alysia McCarthy, Ed Templeton,

Chris Johannson, et. al.—were "Beautiful Losers," we were just losers. Losing was the only way in or out.

You always know what you'll find when you open one of Kevin's chapbooks in the same way you know what to expect when you arrive at the beach: the broken hourglass of time between your toes, the drunken liturgy of waves, a longing to walk out into it and drown or learn how to breathe under water. And you return to them for the same reason: because it's refuge from all the rest.

Anchored in a kind of "surf noir"—a vernacular that's equal parts Venice Beach boardwalk and Palo Alto strip mall, the poems are awash in California patois as far as their temporal particularity—needles, tide charts, neon hangovers in rundown strip malls, wet footprints on baked asphalt. But they always seek a classical and romantic eternality in their visions of place—the muse in a wet suit, Keats' Moneta through a veil of kelp.

If Charles Olson was open field, then Kevin Opstedal is open ocean—the de facto poet laureate of The Great Pacific Garbage Patch. His poems echo, reflect and sing what America has become, its death wish—the empty detritus of Walt Whitman's manifested destiny. They're prophetic laments not for the end of the frontier, but for the lies that got us to the edge of it.

You'll find, too, in Kevin's poems, what Edmund Berrigan used to jokingly call "depressionism." More doom than melancholy, I suspect it was, at least in part, an impending sense that "el tsunami" of professional poetry was about to wash us into oblivion before we'd even paddled out. And I suppose it did.

But here's another wave with this book.

They're still gonna love you in Japan, Kevin. I just know it.

Noel Black
March, 2016
Colorado Springs, CO

for Pamela

I open my eyes
& there you are

I

Porphyry wrote that the generation of
images in the mind is from water

— CHARLES OLSON

Curse of the Surf Zombie

The late afternoon sky was like something
Miss Montana 1979 spilled on her bikini
out near the ice machine
at the Sea Garden Motel
in Pismo
    & the·light was all
        nickels & dimes
                dancing across the pavement
inside the sound of gears grinding
    just a block from the beach

The sunset haze
      reaching for the
            pulse of the tide
                 w/compression dings
                in silver mist
                     propped against a chainlink fence
it was like the Ark of the Covenant
dissolving in a shot glass...

Still there is that light & heavy wind to contend with
& a dusty swimming pool blue turquoise sky rocking
all the way back to the Land of the Dead
w/a few thin clouds feathering out
as though they had something to say but thought better of it

a sheet of silk torn right down the middle

if knowing what knowing might be would make any difference

The tree fern whispers out the side of its mouth like Elvis
in his decline & you set aside the machete
& plunge your wrists into the beaded foam

Seagulls calling from the jetty speak the same language as Aeschylus
though w/an accent that is straight from the surf ghetto

Palm trees hovering like divine scripture
begging for more as if it was the only way to pinpoint the
exact coordinates that will transport us to the
here & now

A norteño accordion tuning up at the bottom of the sea...

Sheet music fluttering in the breeze...

Samuel Taylor Coleridge / Pacific Gas & Electric

Any meaning other than it so encumbers recognition
like a red Corvette driven straight off the pier

"There's more concrete in the world than there are good waves"

I was spilling the last glass of water in California
translated from English into Japanese into Arabic into Klingon
& back into English

"It all makes sense if you stand back & look at it from a distance"

I wore dark glasses beneath a desperate haircut & the
cypress trees were huddled above the beach like the Women of Thebes

(the sky breaking open behind them
partly sunny w/a prevailing sense of impending doom

I had to catch the replay in glorious technicolor
all kinds of low-end torque rumbling in transition w/cracked
bells & clarinets washing up onshore with the incoming tide

A tangle of mist laying flat on the wet sand at the ocean's edge

Maybe you know what I mean. Maybe you've been there.
Playing Parmenides to my Heraclitus. A not quite harmonic
convergence. Drinks were served out on the veranda.
I preferred the rain puddles in the parking lot.

A fistful of sand & a rippling curtain of mist
is about all I'm going to need for the forseeable, I said

Standing in line at the beer store "looming" as maybe Frankenstein's
monster might on a Friday night in S. Cruz. I couldn't begin to tell you
& I won't even try weaving among the shadows. The vault of heaven is
wide open & the stars assume you know the name of every constellation
from Andromeda to Vulpecula, but that doesn't mean you can find your
car keys. The palm trees rattle their bones & a light seabreeze fucking
w/your equilibrium has you doing your best Joe Cocker imitation right
there in the parking lot. Just one of the many obstacles you'll encounter
along the path of least resistance.

Slick liquid neon palette of sunset still lingering in the heavy Pacific sky

X-number of gulls like
        hours, moments, dreams, picking up speed
                & putting it down again

        The fogmist like a leadweight
                        holds the beach in place
                when everything else is falling from your
                                bulletproof kimono

                representing something that will remain
                        casually unresolved
                locked away where the seabreeze goes
                                returning the sky to its default settings

& late night early morning ocean fog swamps the streets

        the wet sidewalk is as dark as your eyes by now

Lights flickering along the pier
already under water

little left to the imagination / more than enough

(you know & I know) the tempo of the Dharma
is not always so easy to dance to

The Temple of the Drama used to be up at
RCA Beach, it was made out of drift-
wood & sand & the vague feeling that we were invincible

if I remember right I held your hand on the way down

& I made detailed drawings of your tattoos but
I can't show them to you because they are mine now
& this is how I will love you

The Tender Distortion
of Parking Lots Near the Sea

Indispensable wet pavement
strumming the latitude & longitude
speaks to the inner noble savage

stars gravitate towards the corners of the sky
      while breath continues to scratch the surface

you get used to it after a while

Trees fall inside tubes
held up against the light

          morning somersaults from the vaulted
          sky ceiling

              wings stroke your left ventricle

The way pavement starts to ripple in the light
the sun creasing the late afternoon sky

              might put a dent in your halo

Banzai Run

Air Bubbles
It's the year 1425, daybreak, at Mount St. Agnes
& you are writing a devotion entitled The Labyrinth of Kindness

yes, the day is new & shiny like the bathroom fixtures at the
Lava Lounge in West Hollywood where tonight the Blue Hawaiians
tune up for the deeply sedated
                        snake-dancing across the linoleum to claim
their little packets of salvation, Jim, you know the old song
lest these portentous clouds part

You wear the avalanche & I sport a fashionable swamp disaster

It is monsoon season

Transition Ritual
The coast is clearing
your sorry rainbow bends
& the moment is too full of
tarnished spoons
strange birds
dogs
sharks
& windswept aimlessness

Night parting the white brick gesture
eucalyptus (a sound)

long silver interludes you empty & reuse on wet Sundays
waiting for the buzz to set in

Banzai Run
Listening to Hawaiian Music by
Warne Marsh & Art Pepper circa 1957
in the Tiki Room off Pacific & Windward
Playa del Rey
         & sippin' at bells betwixt the nightingale riffs
of El Paradiso (no resistance whatsoever, dig)
& in my head there is this sound as of a basketball
being dribbled across the blacktop on a hot August night in 1969
& the moon was a tambourine
laying a little jingle-jangle upon those who would disregard true emotion

The Lives of the Poets

Rimbaud
I always picture him
shooting the rapids
down the River of Forgetfulness

"Keats was a baiter of bears who died of lust"
He said that until now the
earliest hair sample to show
traces of cocaine use
was a lock from the poet John Keats—
Funny, I never figured Keats as the
Hollywood type

Coleridge
I am the honorable
Samuel Taylor Coleridge

don't fuck with me

Rain

A piece of rain hits the pavement
& God scooped from blue horizontal
clear headed & thirsty
Versus the weather I've got ritual
one step forward, two steps back

It's a dance I do
a kind of subliminal watusi shuffle
you'll never see

arcing this tragic sense I have of it all
    in blue shadows that cling

The rain kept being rain
& I kept staring into it
with eyes like forever

Send 50 Beers

I'm going to Tierra del Fuego
I'm already there actually
preferring the fait accompli
to the centrifugal breeze

which is probably a concession to
the gauze-like fluorescence you are bandaged in

premonitions, throbbings & the damage (love)

tumbling into the buffer zone

& I don't want to kill anyone anymore
well, maybe just one guy
& maybe not even kill just maim…

You see I'm nearly a bodhisattva
pounding at the door of unending compassion
with a sledgehammer

A Short History of Surf Music

(Night) & the wind is working in the leaves
manipulative as in April when it's really July
I should have known better than to rerun lost causes now
as the music swells & the credits roll up
I know the pulse these cold fingers search for
is only a ripple on the surface of a black pool   my heart
a stone skipping across the surface of a black pool
bending silver reeds that palpate your aura
My radio indulges in Martian feedback
the hydraulic surge of waves the eye could see
move and
then it's
20,000 leagues beneath the parking lot
with Dick Dale & the Deltones

Albatross Taco

It sounds rusty like an old Buick might
　　if it was a door hinge instead
It's worse when it rains then the dark
　　seeps out under the door & into the street
Might recall some other time like
　　turbulence on the moon
Eyes the color of roadside geraniums
　　see you falling past Santa Monica so tangible
　　unsheathed from 48 hours of silver
I thought it was a neat trick
　　scrolling the sunset like that
& carving back across the face of it
　　like a gull

Full Tilt

1.
The dark reaches
       & the sky bends

The wind rattles dry leaves blown
       clattering over the pavement

Everyone's got their own personal escape route
       so why are my hands shaking?

A tiny blue window opens
       in a corner of the lagoon

Vast Chevrolets cruise the horizon

2.
The stage is set with darkwater angels
resembling nothing so much as
those faceless inhabitants of dreams
who carry messages from deep in there
where the dreaming's stored

One of the last of the
rainy-day women
trudges through the sand

& light fills the air

the air which is slashed by gulls
in my poems

3.
From emerald & steel waves
           clawing at Asteroid Beach
beneath a chrome-plated sun
       gnarly prows of bituminous ruin

Out along the jetty
        made entirely of the volcanic rubble of dead stars
the scuttling spider-shuffle of red crabs
           makes a sound like dry leaves
clattering over the pavement

From the depths of a fatal buzz
    wicked day-glo visions thresh the foam

        the waves charging
           like horses
                into the sand

4.
The sun drops like an incendiary pearl
into the wildly churning sea

There is a certain grace
to the inevitable

it soars in on seagull's wings

it wheels & pivots

& I am bent
into a stupor of rare depth where
silver airships dock

hey hey

loading up
on the chosen few

Live Acoustic Rust

Traffic out on the El Camino Unreal

Waves down at the beach

Wind in the palm trees...

    I thought it was applause

    I thought I should take a bow

Poverty

"Everything belongs to me
because I am poor" that's
Kerouac talking
through the leaky time warp
of the written word

& I can't read that
without thinking of Celine who wrote
"Almost every desire
a poor man has
is a punishable offense"

Stained Glass

The day bends to drink
        from your cupped hands
ocean dark & the wind
                leaning against seaflowers
anxious to tell you something you
        don't want to hear
& so can't avoid

    the waves in this light turning to chrome
(in my head)

            strands of tinsel rain
pasted to a wall of mist
        that falls & keeps falling...

pretty soon you'll feel it

            just when you hoped you'd
        never feel anything again

Apollinaire's Brother-in-Law

Looped & windowed
crispèd & sere
morning glory & tilted

        "a drug induced coma"

top hat
tie
white gloves
a silver-handled walking stick
& pistols at 20 paces

        Sherlock Holmes smoking a long stemmed pipe
        (opium?) one hand held to his chin the other
        dangling

        "Watson!" he cries
        "Bring me an orange soda!"

Dawn Patrol

Waking too early with colors I assume are there
because the sun filters down through irradiated kool-aid

the electric turquoise effect in particular is stunning it squats in my hand
only a few inches above the coast highway

like the patron saint of big waves out there running with the winter swell
or pausing briefly at yonder taco stand to consider the karmic value of

beer for breakfast with Keanu Reeves

Venice

It was that perfect cut of blue above
the faded pink stucco
the sea breeze that came down Venice Blvd
turned left to bend the trees along Lincoln

the tinkling sound
of maybe windchimes
doing their number on you

The old guys all called me "Red"

the other kids knew that I'd do just about anything
on a dare

I climbed halfway up that palm tree

never did come down

Beach Access

Before losing battles I never did want to fight
became my M.O.
                              baby radiance dipped
to one candle
                    said "Don't look back"
                                        if it makes you happy

I once knew light that was grace
with a discerning wit not to be
tread upon in the backyard of my peers

I'm walking 5:00 shadows out to the beach

God was right about love
but I forgot to ask him about his crutch

Tracks

of filtered light
shafting through stained-glass camouflage
drain the sunset
broken up with headlines
of what's lost & won.

I can't call
love
for example turning
her wrists a kind of silver
against the glassy surf the
shimmer of that reflected—

When the wind picks up in the eucalyptus
like a vacuum cleaner surfacing in the South Pacific
I get the bends

White Man, Tomorrow You Die!

1
At the tone the time will be
Folded in like a secret note passed among hands
That tremble slightly darkened as though gloved with shadows
I spill a little coffee in honor of the dead

Stuck in a radiant groove from which shimmers devolve
As if from an immense dripping rainforest
You take continuous soundings
To earn flat white-out days

"I think I'll get a handgun" fades
Into the total lithium vortex
Torn up inside but smiling
A last damp toke divided by 96 tears

I thought I had the resiliency of a cartoon character
But I seem to have been mistaken
About a number of things

2
A loose cloud formation is stashed in a window

                                                in my heart
A wind goes there
                         smoking the remnants of last nights dream
A girl
          who is only tender
                              is
                                    of be-radiant
                                      descending
that expedient empurpled or not at all
                                shade
                                      tinted by the hand of god

& therefore feasible
The soured habitual cream of yesterday
yearning for the virulent privileges of tomorrow
deploys desperation's boomerang

& light is crushed into silver arras of mist
    faded insubstanced dreams that persist

3
The turquoise feather
                falling
                              from the sunset wing
is drifting
is darkening
                near the beach
                          a tree in a shroud of
                          rippling shadow
& everything is bruised

& everything murmurs

a kind of sacred song...
                      it won't be long...
                                  though lately you
"wonder"

(fingers rehearsing a futile caress)
                every day, every night
                          a little less

Seems Like

Whatever I'm becoming it
staggers in puddles of moonlight
lifting its head, looking around
like a man waking up in jail

It comes in waves it's
packaged that way
like seagulls wings like
long cool windshield wiper blades

& you (even you) are sometimes aware

You can live from moment to moment
but between those moments the
gaping maw of the abyss
how can you jump it?

Los Paranoias

I signed up for the coma but
    all I got was short-term memory loss
      & blurred vision

      & now
  seeming déjà vu spanks the cerebrum
    & Space throbs with the tempo of something
      possible as if it was me tapping at the window

my eyes degaussed by a million silicon butterflies
pinned to the icy light

Poem for Carmen Miranda

A dark compassion evaporates
Leaving the pavement warm
& if you put your ear to it you can hear
The forgotten footsteps ringing clear as a moonless sky

Which isn't clear at all is it?

"It's too dark to say"

Diving headfirst into a shadow
& disappearing without so much as a ripple

When I'd rather be visiting the tropical paradise
That hides behind the refrigerator

Where I dance the mambo
with Carmen Miranda
every night

Earthquake Weather

The sky is on the verge of a velvet breakdown
    & you are tuned in to the cosmic radio
which here in Santa Cruz is Eric Dolphy playing
    "Out to Lunch"
I've had a lethal dose of early morning fog & now
    it's time for danger, foretelling & elbow grease
to append to your notes on tango research I last saw
    fluttering in the breeze like
& offering a quick prayer to the Tiki God of Nails
    total destruction & the atomic collage
I scrape the rust off my eyes & stagger into history
    an extravagance I have yet to afford

Distance

Tunnels to the beach for eyes
coasting on tears

or storm clouds parked over Ocean Street when
she finds her fingers hurt

Bending back through the channels of memory
to destroy all traces of you

is too brutal too
essential

Gazing out across the rainy expanse of the Serengeti
to see her posing in the distance

as though I didn't know her

as though I couldn't inventory the contents
of her soul

California Redemption Value

If all we had to contend with here in California
was earthquakes, mudslides, forest fires & disastrous marriages
we could really dance
like a match struck in a monsoon

When El Tsunami finally hits
we'll just bring out the buckets

Everything here is a natural disaster

Everything here is an act of God

100-Year Flood Zone

Empty husks of light rustle among the
silkworms
on the avenue that
winds through the bonsai forest

You are always about a half-an-inch above
the ground
you glide & the
miniature palm trees sway
it's the only way they have of
expressing their disappointment

I thought I saw you
dangling from the edge of some
impossibly high light-fixture
your entourage was suspicious
an anti-freeze aura lit up their
faces so that I had to turn away

partly because my heart
was broken & partly because
these images have already been
incorporated
into a larger picture

one that
no longer
includes you

Needles on the Beach

1./ Once Steve McQueen gets hold of the 12-gauge pump shotgun
in *The Getaway* all prior theories of prosody turn into a thin brown
fluid of some sort.

2./ *Dr. Strangelove*, on the other hand, should be seen on a double-bill
with *The Manchurian Candidate* & the collected poems of
Gerard Manley Hopkins.

It might lead to some mirth.

3./ The last time I had mirth it came with an ankle rash.

3a./– Insert here a vision of St. Jude carrying a water pistol & a
framed photograph of Pearl Buck.

"I don't know man, my heart got lost in transit."

I read "lonely" ocean when the word was "lovely"
(must be something wrong with my eyes, but then, why not
"lonely ocean"?

Bong Water Babies

trident
wheel
horse

How is it your reflection precedes you?

This room here trimmed in black-yellow sunlight
broken glass of angelic origin
bits of rotted cellophane, colored paper, foil
fishing lures? a panorama

plate glass   *regarded physically as*
beach glass   *supercooled liquids rather than*
stained glass   *true solids; a windowpane*
safety glass   *a mirror, a barometer, etc*
art glass
water glass

all of the above shattered

the inner mind, the hidden heart

One More Lilting Adrenalin Riff

Trees sway like an afterthought & the traffic picks up
Murmur of distant sea, pale beneath the haze
Swim out of it in someone else's raincoat
Half-a-pack of cigarettes in yr pocket but no money
And later you might miss the wet leaves clinging to the pavement
You might fade...
You might get tough for a minute then black out to prove
Something about darkness being an emotional response
In permanent rainy neon like gauze
Each moves slowly within
Or tiptoes to the edge of I don't know what darkening

Detour

Standing there at the window
Your eyes like dirty glass & the
Dark tumbles with you inside
& the radio doth play
You know all those forgotten numbers you
Thought you'd never have to hear again...
If you could only blank-out halfway there
Peeling your shadow from the floor
Like all the others fooled into thinking
There's something more when there's only less
As in all you had but couldn't keep
& everything you understand but can't believe—
If you'd never been here
You'd never have to leave

Figure the Cumulative
Effect as Mileage

A tropic redundancy ditches itself at last
in overlapping sheets of clear cobalt

you strike it with a hammer to get that
familiar ring above the mumbling
incoherencies of the swell—

I'm living inside the implications of that

If you detach the wind from the leaves
the ambient long-distance muddy green intervals
haul in forgotten Hawaiian war chants

to body-slam the alluvial symmetry
expressed as a curve reaching up over itself

not quite humanoid enough to talk to

Standing Water

Long full-rail cutbacks
must have looked extra-terrestrial in 1965
Watching the sun dip behind the
evening glass (a reference to
the tide table in my head)
I don't see how I can avoid becoming
just another column of smoke
"the clouds pass by and the rain does its work
and all individual beings flow into their forms"
I guess that includes you & me
in the heavy bruised light of sundown
like it was all retribution & dusted

Aerosol

Fingers unlace forgiveness
pausing for an egg sandwich
& a toke of gravity
hoisted from a recalcitrant passion
I've sworn allegiance to

just as opposable thumbs & the ability
to cry on demand have
set you apart from your neighbor

Captain Cook probably never
thought of himself as "breakfast" either

I'm sloping down toward indecision
& a haircut although I prefer listening
to sand drift along the pavement
that I might feel at least as elusive

Tropical Depression

I go to the window
            comb out my eyes
        try a few abstract threats
pass out
            read Donne, Aquinas & Rimbaud
        play Pipeline   on a banjo   inside a pattern
Everything o.k.
                            my St. Christopher medal
            white t-shirt
                            wonderama
on the other side of gravity

                            Even the trees are thinking about it
        the way a cloud thinks cement

merely sparkling cold
part rainbow part fogbank (beaded fringe)
            sharp edges out of focus
                        against which waves break
        rearranging what I see what I remember

            empty eyes just echoes
            of other eyes

inventing winter in the iron cypress

            & you get that feathery sense everything
            is slightly changed
            somehow

Shitty Dance Music

Her theory was, uh, energy
& why do you wanna go to L.A. for?
an emotional quality I guess I missed
I think it was something from Shelley
that one might toggle back
& forth   accepting Everything Blackened
like teeth   a plate of eleven
all ships   skimming the glass
I see moving   I always knew was something
makes itself plummet
Often I drove past white buildings
out of a book I sold because
I couldn't carry that burden any longer
I sometimes remember equilibrium
and the big X's that crossed out our mistakes

90-percent water

I have pale blue eyes, 3 cigarettes & an unfortunate personality
like Jacques Cousteau
                        & I too have often found myself
gripping the current that carries me
            always just 3 or 4 feet above the spiked
velvet of the ocean floor

. . . .

1.
Everything here emanates from the sea
    and from Hamlet
Every transcendental emergency
    hovering on the horizon just long enough
for me to get a read on it

2.
Neon signatures at the corners of the tide
    that you may conceal
black neoprene   pale diluted sunset
sand crab   seagull   beer can
coral   shell   feather
acetylene taco   broken pieces of
                                  colored glass

3.
Japanese name tags for the Prince of Denmark
    at the water's edge

. . . .
Double Overhead
    That it was the dark voice of the sea that sang
    in kind through the heavy green crash of the
    palm leaves that I drove my fate past
    assuming real estate is still out there

The ocean surrounds us
holds us
cradles us as with
affection

& no chrysanthemums or telephones
ascending to Hollywood

(the ineluctable or
merely sleazy)

The heavy green crash of the sea that sang
in the dark voice of the palm leaves

a darkness like crushed poppies
shadows of heat rising
& rain in thin wires

. . . .

There was a film I saw at St. Mark's Grammar School
that showed white horses charging into the surf
a beautiful image I only recalled 3 years ago in a fever
& then now, as I fold myself into the easy dark,
those horses & the surf...

It may have been raining & the water may have been
dark I think it was filmed in France

all shorebreak & white foam white
horses & the thunder of waves & hooves

A sunset naming the memory in some forgotten language
where I go carrying a flashlight & a wetsuit
still waiting to be tagged with a meaning

Morning Glass

In 6 minutes it'll be 5 days
slamming through the lunar fog
riding the torque of the hummingbird sun
a minor headache in my left ear
& a tremor in my touch...

just a little off, you know, but
still subject to a routine cause & effect
I no longer believe in
beside the subzero telephone
which remains unanswered
because I'm not there

because to be gone is the only vanity I can afford right now

pure blue sensations of day
peel away whatever interest there was in something that fades

& now tilting down into the blue-green concrete Pacific
to measure the evaporation rate
because this breeze will continue to distinguish
gliding out along your flawless rush
to a place where breath alone is no solution
& I break down into interchangeable parts

the air represented by seagulls & a few clouds here & there

so that I might learn their calm

Concrete Submarines

This storm front isn't listed at cumulus dot com
and these winds aren't exactly programmed to
sweep the leaves from the street

There are places we can go if you care to go
always far away, always just right here
meant to realign the stars that failed us

feeling each one burning out distinct
so that I pretend sometimes I'll look up
and see thru the empty sockets of their light

that I might know in all this swirling dark
who you are now & why this is so

Baby Donut

The sagging California light
         yet another dear ex-friend
threatening the world with judgement
            or mercy

But I keep standing here breathing
occasionally
as though waiting for a remedy
that just doesn't exist

saying more or less the idea was a girl
I left unattended

craving an idea of bliss like
turning Coke to Pepsi might cure my narcolepsy
has a weird metaphysical trade-in value

In the movie version she was
a bit more opaque

I found the performance instructive
but fucked up when I took it on the road

Reckoning

You rig up an antenna & point it over the
moon's left shoulder listening in on
a high piano Mass for the rising tide
& Sister Edith Mary
    skipping into the darkness
at 1301 Orizaba Street
    birthplace of radium, gravity & the hook shot

—introspection & dread like
an outlaw plate of thunder food
crashing in through your glassy attention

    long ago signed over to pelicans
    & cormorants wheeling in the
        nonspecific blue latitudes

falling so perfectly across the
rippling pulse of the water
    darker than the night
& when the sun rises
    it's the color of steel

Kahuna Classics. Melodrama. The Shimmy. The Twist. Lyme disease. Etc.

The cosmic lounge act
playing nonstop inside the cells I can feel migrate
from aqua tides dragging up pearls like rosaries you finger

beneath a shallow sky

where the sun has spent the better part of the day proving itself
to the pavement I guess

Such a sad cup to drink from in the end
which is just beginning its
split-second rendezvous with some future life you've
managed to postpone up to now

is stained a nervous blue

the wind cuts through...

It sounds a little like an electric ukulele
you play with your teeth
when you're asleep

Catholic Poem

There's a silver light
slips from the wound

you want to dip your fingers in it
before it disappears...

sand bleached white in its glow

let's assume is precious in its glass-like anxiety

needs someone to blame

...the blood disappointed by the light
blue smoke under a fading sunset

tracing the wound
with a terrible love

In the Wind

She awakens to dreams of
    a desperate nature
        a need to dull all the
sharp edges she's gathered
    along with the frozen
        breath of her lovers
I could watch her take
        her clothes off forever
    wondering if she could
go all the way like
    down to peeling the
        flesh from her body to
reveal her pure white bones
    & then to crush those
        bones into a fine white
powder you could watch get
    blown away in the wind

The flames could be seen for miles

One of the earliest recorded
beach barbeques
was the cremation of Shelley
August 15, 1822
on the Italian coast
between Massa & Viareggio

Whenever I look at Louis-Edward Fournier's painting of it
I always imagine Byron in shades, an aloha shirt
& a pair of board shorts—

A dark ribbon of smoke rising into the dusty blue
indifference of a late afternoon sky

The Cremation of Shelley

after Trelawny

More wine was poured over
Shelley's dead body
than he had consumed
during his life. This
w/the oil & salt made
the yellow flames glisten
& quiver.

The corpse fell open
& the heart was laid bare.

The frontal bone of the
skull fell off
and, as the back of the skull rested
on the red-hot bottom bars
of the furnace, the
brains literally seethed,
bubbled and boiled
as in a cauldron,
for a very long time.

1000 Ships

Like thoughts of the
               sky leaning against
a lone palm
tree

               with a midnight
               sunburn
                         & a deck of cards
lit up like a   string of lights   along the pier
her eyes invisible
                         (green, in the sun)
in the black & white
                                   polaroid snuff shot
          I've got pinned to my heart

Pacific Bell

nasturtiums

gone   }   Ginger Rogers

some kind of fishpond

I never thought about time so much

the wind   warm   whispering
the name of the earth

The last of California leans into the white sky

the beach closed due to something in the water

Residuals

Assuming remote access to where the
shapeless relic of our dissolution will ever
knuckle down or situate these tears with
surgical precision within a closed circuit

nor in disparity to shoulder more various
chemical attributes slipping unnoticed beneath
the machine-tooled arc of sky would be
certain dark reverence to things broken

No I would seal these in the vacuum of
a mock virtue & abandon the wreck at some desolate
interchange thereby reclaiming the neglect
it took so long to perfect if in those distant lights

the glimmering loss of all I thought was mine
proves less the cargo of a chartered voyage
than the scattered remains of moments yet to come

II

"Buddhas and engines serve us undersea"

— HART CRANE

Playa de los Muertos

The inside of my skull felt as though it had been scraped with a table spoon. I spoke to leaves that skittered past on the pavement. Time sped up then slowed down to an agonizing crawl. If it was true that the mind & the body were one then I was fucked. Once on a beach just north of Malibu I left my body for a while I think. I watched walls of sheet glass stand up like vertical swimming pools then crash soundlessly in on themselves. It was all very quiet. The girl I was with said later that she thought I had died. I thought so too but didn't want to say so. She had blue eyes that seemed almost silver. There were broken things in her head. I guess that was something we had in common.

Reef Dance

A Morality Play
1. Out along the crumbling edges of consciousness.
2. Urban beach hassles (a given).
3. Alright. So tremble.

(An allegory)

She disappeared into a cloud of last minute decisions.

17b. Low tide. White mist trailing off the lip of black waves.
42. Shimmering.
43. Bent.

Scene 71. Interior (night).

"There's been a terrible mistake."

1a. She was her mother's sister & her father's brother. It was problematic.

1b. She spent her free time doorbell ditching at the Gates of Paradise.

The Water's End
He said what you need is to read a
really good travel book like Naked Lunch

Memorandum
1. That rogue sunset has got your number
2. and
3. don't ever give your real name.

Fading like a feather of
excess acetylene

Drinking cough syrup with John Keats
in a dream
on the bluff at Pacific Palisades

I can see the little warning lights of madness
flickering in his heavily medicated
bloodshot eyes

& leaning into the cold wind
strains of surf guitar
slicing in off Santa Monica Bay

and so Baja, Punta Baja,
Pipeline, The Wedge, High Tide (by The Lively Ones)
lend a dark twang to the
clear almost perfect blue

as if this wasn't the End of Days

O angel of the abyss

Milarepa filter cigarette

The Complete Collected Postcards

Mickey Dora carried Malibu point
like a leadweight. This is the subtext to
Gidget Goes Hawaiian.

In the tide pools at Leo Carrillo a similar
struggle ensues. Old school.

I figured it to be at least paleozoic.

That is before the advent of a vengeful god
subdivided the beachfront
making sinners of us all.

Over the Edge

Another day made of preternatural acetate
folded to fit every corner of the sky

a kind of see-thru origami

The cool air's acceleration in this light is memory
too early yet to say where it's going
having been there already

I guess it's enough to strike a chord
& follow it on out past the retail outlets
& gas stations glittering like candy wrappers in the sun

Tomorrow's an easy question

today

though paddling up a dark vein like Ponce de León
in the steam-heat tropic inversion dropping down over
the Pacific at this hour (twilight)

& everything clears away from the horizontal
blinded by colors alternating   turquoise / pink / silver

As invariably the darkening clouds obscure
empty blue concepts of sky

the pace & stroke of trees setting the tempo

in that literal & therefore suspect emotion

will burden the restless green ocean water

simulating what I assume to be a kind of

Paleozoic breakdown but gracefully

like clairvoyant with light

inhabited by a similar mis-

conception shivering slow & empty

to be swept up in the thick diminuendo of

mist split by shadows I suppose in

answer dissolving

upon the lips of all those lost

possibilities

& by that resigned to fate

lingering just long enough

to be forgotten

The Drowning Man
Knows His God

Now that you've stalled out
between the slide step & the pivot
              there's nothing left but rain
       & all the doomed bikini dolls
       of El Segundo

2.

              We are near Point Dume
              I wonder if Kathy is still there waiting for
              me I told her I'd be right back

              but then that was in 1974

3.
In my personal doomsday prophecy
                     San Francisco will have to burn again until
a tsunami of biblical proportions
                            douses the flames

& then the New Messiah will arise form the ruins

              they'll call him "Flipper"

Jodie Foster at Malibu

Something really great & pure like a skin rash
   they tell you not to scratch but you do anyway
like hepatitis in a very deliberate red dress
   or the way shadows lay flat on the sand
The sunsets here are famous
   tufts of dry yellow grass growing
up out of cracks in the pavement
   Against similar skies you too might weep
or enter the seminary
   an entire month of summer passing like silk across her thighs
& later having a cigarette for lunch
   her lips the color of faded Seconals
depending on the time of day &
   out the window the only thing I can be sure of is the distance
now that she has developed this sensitivity to the time it takes
   to be here telling me she saw Lou Reed
on the street in his pajamas
   something so tender yet apocryphal I suspect
Just as in New York versus Hollywood the winner is Duluth
   I've never been able to work out a decent rhyme
scheme for a suicide note

He Wanted to Know the Names

Naomi Shakewell

Dean Purple

Beverly Drive

Lefty Heyerdahl

DiDi Lupus

Nadine Lapdance

Leon Tidewater

Little Joe Bloom

Sally Parkinglot

Tyrone Nod

Loretta Spank

Muriel Nitrate

Bikini Sunset

Ape Jackson

Jim Scatter

Frenchy Gomez

Traci Bungalow

Torn Clipjoint

Benny Earle

Yolanda Pipeline

Sunset & Noir

Inside a bottle-cap the sound of waves

On the street every shadow nailed into place

In the palm trees that border the parking lot
the pale eyes of pigeons smack up against heaven

where God crouches
like a mechanic

Goodbye Kodachrome

That was me then as now
plus & minus the 1963 Tijuana Thunderbird
parked forever out where the pavement meets the sea
& the girl who stuck around like hepatitis
with a fistful of loaded fingers
& a shady zip-code
We were right there for a minute or two
but the colors started to fade
even before the snapshot was developed
& that thin shadow filled her shoes
& I cut my hair
& drove north with the radio cranked up loud enough
to drown out the promises that never quite made it

Repeat After Me

The Inventory (within eye-shot):
1. Venice BAMBOO Calif.
    (in script) on the longboard
2. Royal Quiet DeLuxe
3. Pacific Coast Highway
4. HEAVY BREATHING
    (also of the process so inclined)
5. *A History of Violence*

Tracing the shadow of a gull on the sand or
pavement   end of Tokaido Road
Bend, Oregon   spot on scarlet
Santa Barbara
                    roosters crowing across the
Mexican or Guatemalan rooftops
in the vague care of palm shadows, leaf shadow
night of the lunar eclipse...

Pacific Overture

The dragon in the waves is our
connection to the East

The East is west of here

Yeah, Maybe

The tide came in with bandaged wings
& chrome-plated resolve
                        like an excerpt from Lao Tzu's lost thesis
                                            on oceanography
& I passed out
                as though hit with a
                            90 pound opium sledgehammer

                The ocean stuck her tongue in my ear
                & I heard saxophones, mudslides, cypresses & rain

Everything the color of
a Sunday afternoon in September

                        LUSH / LIFE

        A genetic predisposition to
        the rusty shadows of palm trees
        at dusk
                    obscures the crashing
                                bluegreen insistence of
                                            La Pacifica
                    trapped in the measure of that instant

a slow semi-rational tango
I'm almost certain
                        rakes the brain within its groove

The Sinking of the Sushi Boat

Irony is only a passion for details
before either of us knew what that meant

Pretending one was another
or darkness maybe later...

Someone's God always ready with an answer
the wrong answer usually but

you've got to appreciate the effort

Rare Surf, Vol. 2

The Collected Poems of Arthur Rimbaud
Some pearl dust you peer through
& maybe breathe in a little now & then
switching on the porch lights of X-ville
in your head
feathery surf revisited

Tuesday last (the Feast of St. Samurai)
The sun peeling away the layers of ocean fog
for those who come here to die
1) in dreams half-formed, or
2) in the vacant lot behind the taco stand

Springtime in Purgatory
When an ambulance passes you say a prayer
while I figure someone just got lucky

With absolute zero reading on the consciousness meter

I was thinking of John Donne
doing the handjive

out on the pier
in a dream

where the pavement
turns to sand

& Bukka White
taught me slide guitar

Ripple Effect

Put two & two together
& forget they keep adding up. . .

     The ritual midnight
          alive in the shadow you carry
               thru the streets

such is the nature of loss inverted

to sustain my vehicular
isolation a particular
moment otherwise collapsed
          & like the mist of all those former
expectations dissolving
             long strips of ocean
light
          this morning lifts
that too without measure

This sense of a dark focus
inside it

Blue windows. Green windows. Light. And dark.

     things that flicker on the surface. . .

It's true a semi-Peruvian shot at delirium's all

I've got but like a test
pattern trembling on the viewing screen of
self-indulgence with rain
    & winds clocked at 35 mph
out of the west

      an oblique reference & disembodied
like palm trees at dusk

The panorama of knee-jerk existentialism, sun tan lotion
& dread
      fill our days here the
hand/eye coordination the depth
perception in memory of St. Cadillac
       parked in the moonlight at Point Dume
& always a step or two behind
    the slant of violet tides where
   even now you cultivate the rust of dreams

Tiny Bubbles

She ditched the cigarette
        into a blue expanse.
The gesture was reminiscent. The
        light, a tragic crystal façade,
                read like April in the cuts.
She spoke church latin. Mea culpa,
motherfucker. The plum
        tree in blossom dropped white
                petals in the courtyard.
I heard each one hit the ground.
                She tried to tell me something
        but it was too late. I just couldn't nail that
transposed circuitry to
        disqualify the somber drizzle & the
bells. She folded her shadow
around me. I never learned when
to say when.

Turning Left at Jerusalem I Drove Straight into the Heart of Darkness (Fresno)

Morning drifts of dark cloud meaning fog but
lifted up off the pavement like Sonny Liston that time in Memphis
& his eyes were bright as 7 new pesos
although he was beaten & he knew it.
An orderly universe might be one that includes a cup of coffee
& a slice of pie every now & then.
"Doom & Rain: The Autobiography of Redemption"
rings so true my teeth hurt.
You are a legend now, not only because your curve ball doesn't break but
because you have been knee-capped by "The Poems".
The dirty gray palm trees here are leaning hard into Eternity
like a skinny band of thugs whose luck has just run out.
That's what I like about certain zones of California—
they remind me of Mt. Sinai on a Saturday night.

Some Get Translucent

Like that night in San Francisco
staring at a blank wall wondering
who would be the first to blink

Another night Hermosa Beach when the
mist cleared it was Santa Cruz & I was
still hung-over

the V-dub burning oil

I had a pair of shoes that were
made out of linoleum or something
& an Aloha shirt that should have been
strangled at birth

I quoted Shakespeare to the girls

I guess it should have been Keats

There's no such thing as total
darkness is there? just inky Eternity
full of holes

Hollywood

for Miguel

Jack London lion breath
over cerveza y conch (conch)
at an undisclosed location in central amerika
(tentative title)
rears its heavy heart & holds it aloft like a flag
catching the late medicine winds of sundown
interleaving the trace elements
of a sporadic lucidity leaning up
against the vast tidal sweep.

Volcanic temblors in a dirt floor cantina
at 2:00 in the afternoon of a dusty future where
you carry a .45 automatic & some prayer beads.

Cables connecting
personal blood ties & the visions elicited by them
are the kind of road songs
Deke Thornton forgot to telegraph Townes that night in El Paso.

The señoritas flashing their thighs in the damp moonlit streets of
eternality & salvation.

Yeah.

I'm slamming sideways on a pint of amber,
not scoping the horizon for auras nor annotating the
greater narrative & lyric payload,
but tipping my consciousness to the Dark Lord
I buy a one-way ticket
to Hollywood.

For Anselm, Jane & the Shape-Shifters in the Backyard

"The Poems" done buckled under
a line of coke
    that wasn't there
we had other fish to burn
       & imitation basmati rice
a medium mushroom jail cell
    we shall escape from
      in time

Diesel heat in Colorado
    but already skating my way back to
California in my head
      carrying along with me
Crime School, The Bhagavad Gita,
Aloha Blues

& a little leftover Ezra Poundcake

Underwater Ballet

I had some other place to be. There were complications—
the rooms were too large, the stairway too steep, the walls
were caving in around me.

I had a rope-ladder in order to exit via the window
which was only about 3 stories up but slanted out at a 45 degree
angle over the rocks & the sea below.
Halfway down the ladder I realized how ridiculous all this was.

I stood in a darkened parking structure smoking a cigarette.
A woman approached me to say that she didn't need any matches.
As she walked away I noticed that she had a tail like an alligator
dragging on the floor behind her.

In Mexico I
looked down from a stupendous height as a group of children
gutted & skinned some kind of water buffalo.

In the room next door it was a rainy morning in Seattle.
A naked woman drank coffee from a very ornate antique cup
made of a mysterious metal that changed shape as she sipped from it.
It was distracting but I still wanted to fuck her.

I was accused of a crime I knew that I didn't commit
but the evidence was so overwhelming I began to
question whether I had actually done what they said
& inexplicably forgotten all about it.

I had a job shaping boards at a surf shop in Ventura.
My skin was coated in a thin layer of fiberglass dust.
I had just won the Nobel Prize for literature.

I've never had a dream in which I could fly.
I know that many people share that dream of
flying bird-like high above the earth.
The closest I get is a kind of levitation
where I rise up only a foot or so above the ground
in an upright position
& with an extraordinary amount of effort
manage to glide forward for a few yards before
dropping back down onto my feet.

It's a very difficult & exhausting exercise
& although I must have dreamed it hundreds of times it
never gets any easier.

I've had dreams in which others fly.

Sometimes they sprout wings & take to the sky,
other times, wingless, they just seem to
swim through the air.

Mutiny on the Bongos

The syllables of your breathing tumble
past the freeze-frame sunset
            & I'm wired to the black hole of
      Chinese take-out
pulling the wool over yr rose-colored
goggles
         the way temptation buzzes yr snap decision
            a circular motion that tastes like rain
       inside a rush-to-judgement beer can sonata
but yr blue blue temple
            & coal black silver doesn't really explain the
       bulletproof lingerie
nor those whirlpool eyes shedding their neon tears
          behind dark glasses
            like a Kung-Fu schematic
      of the perfect crime

Endlessly Rocking

The ocean waves never sleep
    They suffer from an epic insomnia
Inconceivable to mere mortals
    Crashing surf music
Roaring out of a car radio
    That picks up the pre-Cambrian
24 hours a day

Poem Near Dusk

Maybe it's just the light against your cheek that
bids my heart unlooked for consent
                    the vestiges of a dull pain gliding pale
      as if a swanlike passion could rake the
            dark trees swaying in your eyes
glassed in & remotely queued to
            a blank space where God wrote "SKY"
conveying a lethal content
            sacred & precise though
      no more than falling expressed
                  by the eyelids primarily I think
& so my heart like a mechanical
      toy sounding distant & hollow
(it seems) in another room
      or in the hands of a cool abstraction (you) nervously reflected
on the surface up until now the way the sky
      inadvertantly empties
            into that which is radiant
                  w/like rays of sunset skating the
                  incandescent tension of silver tides

Liquid Sky

for Pamela

Shadows fall across the threshold of sunset
to sucker punch the ocean fog
launching transparent gray clipper ships
into the June gloom...the space between each wave
the trough the
lull
& in the gathering darkness your eyes

I suppose I'd rather stay here a while after you
leave knowing you'll return
the same but different

& that's the closest we'll ever get to understanding

Along with further subsidiary resolutions to bend in the wind of things
such as they are
I imagine contrary to "the life of the mind"
27 miles of unspoiled seashore that exists only in my head
where it rattles around with other debris
making an awful racket
disturbing the diaphanous membranes
of the dryads, nymphs & mermaids who populate my darker dreams

lighting left-handed cigarettes

& the day is turning to *Night in Tunisia*
as I glance out the window

a page torn from "Varieties of Eucalypti"
flutters in the wind
all green & silver & smelling like coughdrops
that evaporate in tide pools
like clipper ships in the fog of another world

which is here   waiting
for you

19th Century Tattoo

I like that telephone
pole silhouetted against the
blood-orange sky

It's reminiscent of the
crucifix
& seems to hold dark suggestions of
spiritual transmission
& lost phone calls

      in road-to-Damascus-revelation terms

                via the PCH

& whatever's left skids past the
rainpuddles & mudslides
to assert a valerian sense of
what's lyrical
on a one-string ukulele banjo

I heard "whores"
when you said "horse"

        (Book of Revelations, 6:8)

It might have been an appaloosa
& a trail of wreckage

The straight-edge & the automatic
                (pearl-handled)

It's all in the flow
by which I mean the
fluency
& the numbers
of what could be said

. . . .

REVELATION

The light of day was on her

It was night

Half jagged, half ocean smooth

To exaggerate
with a dark heart upon the burning deck of triumph & loss
some regulation size regret
dalliance & indifference, etc…
The day turning a golden bright gray   *in Bolinas*
the sea becoming one with the sky as in a dread pantomime
to be anxious with light & the cascade
more an incidental than reflected elegance may allow
along with traditional applications
I felt that I was perhaps distracting or distracted
something only momentarily real & at that even
only marginally so
but the little altar to Philip (Whalen)   *in the kitchen of*
the photograph, the incense & the turquoise   *Joanne & Donald's*
ring   *house*
in mid-air on ocean
& I almost forgot to add & subtract the variables
Awake too late for coffee & transition   *the day before*
to piece together a consciousness &
attention
nothing there but that isolate incriminating sun & sky
& then several ways to avoid it
feeling just as elemental & star-crossed as anything else here
Andean flutes & toy pianos along with feedback from an electric lyre
Tales of Brave Ulysses or Bodhidharma or someone
trembling
fingers point to the twig jumping in Arthur's hand   *Arthur Okamura*
Do you think the eucalyptus & bamboo care that there's just no
parking downtown? In the midst of doom & rain
I anticipate enchantments

Cadillac to Mexico

We are as clouds that veil the 11:00 News, applying pressure to a
ruptured artery, stripping the paint off a 50 gallon drum full of Marlon
Brando's performance in *On the Waterfront*. The chainlinked molecules
of spring are waiting with crowbars & baseball bats. That was back
when I wore bellbottoms & beads & hung my head in shame. I thought
I had to explain myself as though there was still something left to prove.
My mistake. I meant to say *Last Tango in Paris*—the final scene shot
in a parking lot in Juarez just south of the Olympic Blvd off-ramp.
November had sliced the ankles of the moon. Wind thrashing in the
trees the way a drowning man might gasp for air drawing in a lungful of
water. And in April we drove out to the beach to poison ourselves with
the sunset.

Slow Ride South

Reinventing the
heavy silk of twilight
                    except for the hammer
cypress & wind

                              An imaginary green wreck
quite seriously

African violet telephone
                                   for flute & oboe
               lots of air

DETOUR (for two)

          "I had a blade in my pocket
          there was $500 worth of pills
          in the glove box & the clutch was slipping"

San Luis Obispo

smoke   "Isn't there
& mirrors   an easier
                        way out?"

     (indigo, silver, orange & blank)

one asks & is so rarely answered

The Stumble

You slap yr money down on the coffin lid
& these tear-stained bikini blondes
drop in out of the pale blue nada

it's like spilling a bottle of broken pills

The days here are measured out in thrills per minute
beneath an indiscriminately azure sky
w/a terminal case of the shakes

Cut Glass

A star in the middle of the desert with a lone
railroad and two empty riverbed…like Zuma
Beach scripted thus has a seriously deep radio heart
It gives me the shakes, I have rogue epiphanies
but not enough wah-wah not enough dense blue smoke
If you could ship it out to a beach I know just
north of Santa Cruz then I could
retire there with "The Poems" & die like a man
In the meantime a slight deviation is in order since
even natural history is flush with non-negotiables

Cruise Control

Vacuum Advance

Watching the genius of dark clouds rolling in

I guess we all need to learn something mechanical

& savor someone else's darkness

for a change

Lost Weekend

The trees are throwing shadows back

into the white sky where

God has gone to sleep it off

Close Your Eyes

I'm trying to read her lips

over the telephone

Liquid Drāno

It's as if a switch has been

flipped on and there is now a brain disease—

the waves turning Japanese—

& all that rain drawn up into the syringe

of twilight

Up Against It

Dark paddling all night in swamp dreams
but now there are signs of immaculate
recovery
       sacrifical lung matter
     silver-studded phantoms
          & holy grails

sure, the symptoms are ominous
but we are ominous as well
like seven Eskimos & a backhoe
crossing the border of your disputed consciousness

          I slipped beneath the spell of "The Poems," or rather
          "Los Poemas," & while there I
          picked up a pair of brass knuckles
          & some shin-guards

which means something on the Venice pier (or else)

I was wearing a replica of the Montgomery Clift death scene shirt
& you were decked out like Shell Beach in the fog

      which is shorthand for pale light dropping in from
            what the ancients called "Golden"

Bird of Passage

Awake

the fingers

on her eyelids

drum the light

back

down where

her otherwise conscious

mouth

(tongue, lips, teeth, lies & kisses)

tastes the

powdered

edge

of dreams

Smog Lines

When Juan Rodriguez Cabrillo spotted the brownish haze of Indian fires hanging above the hunting grounds of Southern California, he gave the name Bahia de los Fumos (Bay of the Smoke) to what was either the bay of Santa Monica or San Pedro. Four centuries later, on July 27, 1943, under the front-page headline: CITY HUNTING FOR SOURCE OF 'GAS ATTACK,' the Los Angeles Times reported the fourth assault of a "smoke nuisance." A year later, on September 18, a new word passed into the local lexicon when the paper, using an expression common in Pittsburgh, referred to the bronze pall as "smog (smoke and fog)."

An itemized list:

1 BUSTED SURFBOARD

9 ALLEGORICAL ALLUSIONS

A MILLION RUSTY SUNSETS

4 SYRINGES

7 EMPTY CUPS

3 TRUCK TIRES

56 TOGGLE SWITCHES

19 PLASTIC FLAMINGOS

278 HEROIC COUPLETS

*zero gravity & ghost trains
in the 32 chambers of my heart no less
with last ditch Hail Marys
warbling in a darkness all their own*

        & a particular moment otherwise collapsed
among the pale faint water-flowers
                that pave the memory

I ended up with the bent spoon
& a lifetime subscription to
the sky over Hermosa Beach

(some lives are meant to be
w a s t e d

The Code of the West

Cigarettes
This former junkie standing outside the
    rehab center on University says
"Gimme one of them cowboy killers"
    Another guy calls them nails, says
"Gimme a nail" or
    "I gotta go pick me up a pack of nails"

El Watusi
Mike in
Boulder calls says
Hey
this is Mike
in Boulder
How do you spell
Peloponnesian?

Floating Cowboy Hat
Another code of the West might be
    going so far west you're east
so that riding off into the sunset in Tombstone
    you break on through to morning
in Nagasaki

Fadeaway

We'll wait until we hear the ocean
recite its secret alphabet

Me in my dark robes & you
wearing the standard issue
seaweed & pearls

The sun dragging through the
sky the mists of time clearing
just a little bit...

nothing you haven't already seen before

sinking to the bottom of all this
darkness
means it's still dark but
gets darker

like a ukulele solo gone bad

our fingers had a purpose then
like leaves falling or wings

& the sound of waves
told us everything we
never wanted to know

The Morning Report

Moved heaven & earth.

Got up early to check conditions:

a chilly 58 degrees

clear sky w/a few wisps of feathered clouds

offshore wind

light & variable

waves 2 to 4 feet

sectioning into cauldrons of milky foam

the ocean sloshing up against the horizon

Playa San Pedrito

In Baja there is a bird that sings

"Bring It On Home"

just like Sonny Boy Williamson

Exchange Rate

Laying in bed my eyes lock in on the
thatched palm branches which
form the roof of this casita

I'm trying to translate the pattern into
a language

     The surf thundering the
              tide's coming in

I keep thinking about Rimbaud

Los Oxidados

Shooting pool in a dirt-floor cantina
    "Mucho calor"   yeah, weather's hot, amigo
Dogs wandering in & out of the place
    (they have a little Baja all their own)

Back in the car we take off with the windows rolled down
so that the heat off the blacktop can blast through us

Are those band-aids on the crushed bumper of that '84 Chevy compact?
It rattles & spews dark clouds of smoke
                into the deep blue Mexican air

Mariachis taking a break at the Tecate Six in Pescadero
            Federales hanging out at the corner

Turn left off the highway onto a dirt road
    bounce along through agricultural land
peppers, avocados   palm trees
        veer right at the thrashed VW van
    & roll on out to the beach...

Standing in the shorebreak   intense undertow but
                    the waves are clean
We are as the haze
        ignited by the setting sun

    Shelley must have lived like this on the Mediterranean
    only the waves weren't as good

The Sound of Glass Breaking

A morning dark w/rain
crossing the border
leaving tracks in the mud & sand

the only evidence that we'd ever been here

& I memorized her fingertips
        the lucid & the profane
                        typecast
        everything I ever whispered

& I lost 40 dollars at a dice game I
didn't understand like
crossing the magic
line that separates
a buzz from a hangover

why bother to explain the obvious

        A bad moon rising & traces of silver yet
                        in the blood

as was promised...
                        but one Delta-style
        slide guitar blues number
                recorded in Memphis
        lifted a corner of the dark

The voice of God on cropduster radio

& with a blown gasket on a remote stretch of coastline
sharpening the edge of azure that tipped the horizon
snagged in the teeth of cactus—

    I just sat there staring out at the water
                hypnotized
                    but safe behind dark glasses
singing "My Catatonic Baby" in the slow
                breaking arc of sunset

something antagonistic & pure resolved in that

or so I was told
            the exception
            coursing through yr veins
cut with silver
    (remember?)

& a flickering neon light
                dark blue almost purple
    churning
            out along the point

Odysseus on the PCH

No longer a question of one place
anymore than another
bajo las olas & a vision of that dark
as much a reflection of what I have become as the geographic
      circumstances of my Elizabethan coastline
where the Japanese fog tastes
like tequila
          & 60 miles down the coast
    in the dark
              with one headlight & no brakes
gunning it past the Midnight Taqueria (Pollo del Mar)
                  & Last Gas Discount
flooded in a strange fluorescent light
        wherein you cannot cast a shadow
              is all they will know
an unanswered voice & numb fingers to replicate the exact touch
        as maybe the caress of the tide…

All night long the sea from which the rain is quote
Love made known
        so that the Earth might speak, Ocean
sing

Satan Stole My Surfboard

My heart turns to glass against the
abalone twilight
      set as secret coinage
a folded concrete seacliff lament
    back among those mile-long shadows
bronze-edged in memory now
      making it easy to forget

& though you can't see them
    lost souls fly in V-formation
in a part of the sky
      dreamed on either side of that
humming interference
    buried in the sand
hollowed-out green ocean steel
      to rattle them reliquary bones

When the sun slams down behind
      the razor-feathered turquoise crest
of the last wave
      a fine mist of haze will cancel your eyes
as your precious adrenalin simmers
on the lid of the tide

Turning Silver

In the Dark
These empty streets hum with the echo of traffic that's ringing deep
inside I guess so that they seem to work like a tuning fork that was
struck hours ago but still vibrates a barely audible tone. I figure if you
held a piece of this broken concrete up to your ear you'd hear the roar of
distant engines.

El Camino Unreal
The sky bends down to touch the pavement. Night folds in the corners
of forever as the clouds extradite rain puddles from Honduras. But it's
the edge of California like Kyoto or Chapultepec for all I know hung up
in the dark with rain— like Tangiers—and I'm striding through it in a
leaky black hat...

Directions to the Night Palace
Head west on Sunset and turn left at the whale skeleton. Keep driving
until you get to a dirt road. Continue on for about a mile until you see
the temple ruins then turn right. At the streetlight make another right
& then a quick left. Go down about half a block. There's a pillar of flame
out front. You can't miss it.

Calculated Risk

She knew dark corridors where
she could listen to her pulse beat against the walls
could feel
     her eyes
           amidst clouds
as if she could cast her shadow over the waves
lifted
    is soft
        partially disclosed

but death's tunnel thru a sea shell
obscure realm of tilted altars
          beneath the tidal tremors
      an inconsistent harmony
              extends

like a wind that teases a song out of glass birds
& out on the horizon there was nothing
only the moon
    breaking
        across the water
to enter the wave of it
     or to deliver light
whose fingers initiate the mercenary breath
   in shallow ocean pools
     the color of tarnished mirrors

Prelude to a Quaalude

Remote Control
To sip from the clouds in pursuit of
  some radiant similitude
resulting in the loss of 20% of one's brain cells
  is an even trade-off
considering the alternative

(Detail) The Heaven of the Contented
Palm trees stooping beneath the weight of
a hazy, indistinct concept of Paradise

Midnight at the Lava Lounge
All you're left with is
  a duet for surf cello & diesel engine
white stone wings
  & an 8x10 glossy photo of
the thin hours before dawn

Small Change

A splendid day

To get out in it

————————————

Baudelaire / bottled beer

————————————

Open yr eyes
    all three of them
(blue)

The Mockingbird is My Nightingale
for Pamela

I dreamt I heard a
mockingbird

I dreamt you heard it
too

it made you laugh

I looked at the alarm clock
it was 5:05 a.m.

I said "The mockingbird is
my alarm clock"

"What are you talking about?"
you said

"What mockingbird?"

Selling a Kidney on eBay

for Duncan McNaughton

Two is extravangant when you can
get by with one. Duality is a con-
venient excuse for all kinds of
nasty business. The moral exception
explained in a TV infomercial I never saw
flickers like a blue wing in a blue
sky. Singing the blues. Blue Hawaiians.
Deep blue sea. I was standing on the
bluegreen steps of the Tsunami Palace
smoking a turquoise cigarette—
actually I was smoking two of them
simultaneously
while marveling at the symmetry of it all.
You were carrying a blade that looked like
a silver gull wing & I was stirring my tequila
with a nail.

Smack Up (a romance)

bubble   glass   anemone   stone   sand   shell   rust   slime

spray   kelp   agate   seagull   neon   wave   barnacle   pearl

algae

eelgrass   From over yonder the traveling

turquoise   circus & the seagreen mermaid

cellophane   w/smeared lips & tequila earrings

starfish   These are the days of thread & gravel she

coral   says like Mexican hula stripes on the hood of a

beer can   suicide Chevelle

driftwood   All that tell-tale signage & reprisal

concrete   you know? Furious windchimes of fingerbones &glass

jade   hang from the palomino sky

tar   & just a step away from your tambourine

emerald   balcony the tattoos & clarinets rattle palm trees in Arabic

w/bended knees

Seaslug Duckwalk

Get woozy
Catch hepatitis from surfing
Pull an all-nighter studying for your blood test

The weather made me hungry
so I poured a drink I could wade through

When I stepped into the light
my hair grew crooked

& the day slipped from my hands
the way the tide takes a little slide step
& you grind your teeth instead of breathing

Dancing into the sand

Suffused in bygones, all waving & unused, I drove as far as that '64 El Camino would carry me. It died an untimely death in the Mississippi mud & I left it there. I wound up selling my surfboard to a black lady in Jackson. I think she was psychic. I shuffled around for about a month until I felt the Pacific calling me back & so the road. A nightmare bus to Baton Rouge & the thumb from there to Houston & somehow further. A badass vato on meth wanted to kill me in Las Cruces.

Maybe he did.

I can't remember.

Albuquerque looked like Dakar at dawn, or Juárez at nightfall. I remember spending a night in Tucson. There were locusts as big as your foot wandering the streets & climbing the old adobe walls & cinder block. The stars crashed down into abandoned Navajo pagodas where Keats died. The plastic minimarts selling pulque & beef jerky & fuck magazines. You just have to keep walking. Bullet holes in the roadside saguaro. Bullet holes in discarded beer cans. Bullet holes in everything, including the sky.

I had a long conversation with a lizard outside of Tempe. His eyes were the color of a rained-out weekend & he quoted William Blake. After a while he scampered off into the brush & I caught a ride to L.A. with a drunken Mexican & a whore from Vegas.

They were in love.

Chinese Algebra

That you render the silver
thread of dawn
with unerring fingers strumming the lead edge

tapping a dark vein
& all the broken promises
we've had to plow through to get here

Knowing the fatal intimacy of a bent
fender rattles in the stoke of too many perfect
days strung out along the shore I thought
leaves a little something for the soul to feed upon but

swept up in that rush & outside of time
limits the scope of your tender indifference
& drags the sky away from the horizon
at the winged insistence of gulls

for example

to qualify your absence
even before you turn to go

Placed against the edge of your breath
w/scant fearing
                    gust nor gale force would subsume
& by this random steps & redefines

the way it falls…

      I should know better having reconvened
          to sift horoscopes & bend the tide
    lifting that consolation to accentuate
         your stark confines & rippling pavement

I guess tinseled waves
      or folding sheets of bluegreen
glass when seen from outside
    section the predetermined measure
                 of your pulse

as you reach the end of something you
never even knew began

Allegory & Ode (Condensed)

for Fast Eddie Ainsworth

A bus ticket east is the
Code of the West & the grass
grows all the way to China

450 Bus Miles

Robert Creeley, 1926-2005

The passage a bridge
from one to an-
other
   & in that transfer the
broken syntax
    & a final exit in
Odessa fucking Texas

    as it was given him
or else that grace to
   be relinquished & why
not throw down a few
    against the darkness

for love

Source Code

Near Myth
The all night girls
out on the mainline
muttering the lyrics
What are they nymphs?

Text
"at Ankor Wat
a Hindu myth carved in stone
shows a tug of war
between gods & demons
w/a serpent as a rope. A sea of
milk is churned by this action
& voluptuous women called apsaras
take flight from the froth like
bubbles from champagne"

The Classics
One thing's for sure those
naiads & water sprites
lounging at poolside
will dive into their shadows
one day
& never resurface (although
the cinematic flutter
of their eyelids will
linger

Salt Water Credentials

Green sea opaque
as cumulonimbus
gilded above

the trip
wire of the
tide
you back into

opens
a silver door
in yr head

something the surf said
claiming to be more than
incidental music

like the decline of
civilization as we
only got the introductory
speech in The Odyssey

an expurgated bit like a
bad movie like all the
bad movies laid end to end
spliced together makes
one epic bad movie

but good movies too

Sal Mineo in Siberia
with Judean sideburns

or Johnny Depp shipping out
with the Kwakiutl (or were they
Yurok) northwest coast Indians
with those funeral boats decked
out with feathers & tobacco

cans of pineapples
swiss army knives
fuck magazines & matches

all gifts to the Great
Spirit who doesn't live in the
sky but in the sea

ideas of heaven are
always skyward why?
when the gods all live in the
ocean & we know it

This movie is mostly
green but shot in
black & white
like Auguries of Innocence or
The Gates of Paradise

III

and out here poets sleep beaches all day
with fears of Japan where bronze children
start landslides on their brains

— JIM CARROLL

Truth as History,
or An Ode to Medicine
for Lewis MacAdams

Whatever happened to the blue sparkle
dancing across the water?
 The Adoration of the Magi
      if you want to get technical
   & who doesn't?

I got the bongos but not the sunset

  plus an empty jar of vaseline
  & a voodoo doll in a grass skirt

"Priests and magicians are used in great number"
saith the *I Ching*

It melts in your brain
not in your hand

The puzzle pieces are all
right where you left them

        try to remember the connection

    an apparition   green, translucent

      "indulgent & huge"

but pouring water was I still just a memory?
How was I to know? The
        dragon in the waves breathing fire & great plumes
of mist in the Manchurian surf almanac
                on the shelf
            next to *Hawaiian Mythology* & an empty
tequila bottle (Cabrito Reposado)

The sky's overcast
        velvet, or cement
      the air is moving left to right

        sea lions had wings once

Correspondence

I was wearing a tombstone t-shirt
& a pair of graveyard shades
when I pulled in to the Dream
Diner outside of Barstow

The waitress showed some mileage
but poured a good cup of coffee

There were prairie oysters on the
menu & I asked her about them
"They'll put lead in your pencil,"
she said,

"if you got anyone you
want to write to."

Street Legal

Something swims out of the diluted plasma
of the western sky (pink
is the new blue) the answer to the question "Why not?"
on the tip of my tongue, 96 *Tears*,
THE LONG GOODBYE, a skatewheel, a
pelican, the silhouette of a smile
        in the backseat of a murdered-out Chevy Malibu
& the rusty nail that makes my heart jump when you
slide into a barefoot tango that carries you smack into the vanishing point
& beyond
        where you sleep standing on your head, counting the
money you don't have
        w/a picture of what drowning really looks like
tattooed on your instep

You Do Not Have to Be Present to Win

In the empty street lit by the
flickering red neon
of a motel vacancy sign
no one was there to
hand out tickets to the people
of the future
who are destined to study
Arts & Silences
in the abandoned swimming pools
of deserted homes

(I Think I'm) Surfing Japanese

Prophecy like pure chance
resulted in Medusa & the two-way mirror
Delphic shadows on the boardwalk
& the cigarette I didn't smoke on the pier that night

Her hair like dark water crashing against the jetty
drenched in corrugated steel

& with dripping steps up the ruined concrete stairway
back to the overlook parking lot
a heel of sidewalk groaning with albatrossian hang-time
to hold abeyance with sunset hardware
& a grip of dreamless blonde sand

All the baptismal vestments
& drugstore sunglasses required to perform ablutions
pouring water from a plastic gallon jug over my head
before peeling off the black neoprene & throwing on
t-shirt, shorts, sneakers, sweatshirt against the chill
rips & blades of cold air knifing the damp

Who did it matter what incumbent gloom attends
with a feather of mist tuning E-strings in
the eucalyptus

Dusty murmur of ragged palm trees attending

like the brainchild of silence & slow time

Narrow Margin

It was Mexico at last
mapped in dusty miles of gray
light, silence & iron-lungs.
From where you are to where you
may be going. No way to tell.
"Do you know this road, señor?"
What's there to know.
"A pinched Medusa, freckled with trail dirt
bitchy light years from Anne Frank."
She carried a pistol. My words are just
an extension of this. And so it read
"Palm trees grow in poor soil. They
seem to prefer it." I figured it was
a learned behavior. A shrug as if to
say there's nothing that can be done
about it so why try. The miles grind away
your heartfelt resolutions until all that's
left dies out like a struck match. Cerveza,
por favor. Tequila, pulque, mezcal.
A blown muffler, a burned-out piston.
"El corazón, otra vez?" The journey
ends in bloody disarray, tarnished pesos
& lapsed prescriptions. Tibetan postcards
sent from New Orleans. A sunset
shimmering on a city so far off we can
only imagine.

Center of the Universe

It's damp out there
& either damp or not in here
with drizzle bells & chapstick
& why not good & evil
        & the national debt
      attaining that rarified number of the infinite

as in how many buddhas can park themselves
in the needle's eye
        perfected beneath a long flowing gown
made of quarter-inch steel & seaweed

& stepping out from behind that smokescreen
into thin layers of bluewhite haze back home in
Venice

    the pavement throbbing beneath your sneakers

beach traffic using up all the available metaphors
        before you can wipe away the tears

questionable sunlight crumbling around you

It was always that way

    I was lucky to have been there

when will I ever leave?

From My Chinese Novel

No recourse as choice
is our burden

& the one voice
snapped in two
by words so blessed

or cursed
to go on this way

invents its own
retribution

A man walks into a bar
carrying an octopus

1. Several tons of damp not to mention sun tan lotion
2. Steeped in heavy breathing
3. Beneath a miniature bamboo umbrella
4. A shadow among shadows
5. With bruised knuckles & a book of matches
6. A thin layer of smog caressed by a silver blade
7. Twisted palm trees sipping at the pale sunlight
8. The color of a Japanese wrist
9. A sea swamp veneer accentuates the tattooed hula doll
10. The fishbone tuning fork halo effect
11. Wrecked on adrenaline & perfume
12. Fevered lips stung by salt spray lifted from the marathon tide
13. At the mercy of accelerations
14. & the vicarious hips of parking lots near the sea

All the heavy action was underwater

The stretch of sky
        eternal enough
w/compression dings
where Manjusri hangs w/St. Augustine

Boulevard Insurgentes

in Tijuana where for a few pesos
        the dark night of the soul
            can be all yours

Bienvenidos
you sons-of-bitches

walking across in prison-issue
        huaraches that never quite touch
the ground

Water on the Moon

Double Down

Breath's journey into sleep infected by too many cures still doesn't mean
we'll spin the residual jolt gone hollow where your silk-weaving eyes
torqued the lyric vibe. We found our way out by the light of your cell
phone, the indigenous lord have mercy, & painkiller-grade Tecate. Once
you realize where you are it's where you were & there's no going back.

Liquid Assets

The sand plunges beneath the waves here. Tidepool mirrors exaggerate
the emptiness of the washed out sky. Plastic bottles tangled in dried
out garlands of seaweed & copper wire adorn the water's edge. This
is either the beginning or the end of something, take your pick. The
light is fluoresecent & saturates the beach so that there are no shadows.
Underwater you'll find the shadows of those that have drowned & the
light is turquoise like the windows of a Mexican church.

Somehow Lifted

Drifting through the drugstore parking lot aching for a little voodoo
face-time I had assumed the role of a no-credit editor of silence inside
a forklift catalog of sunsets. A hybrid Day of the Dead tattoo fading
into a sunburnt shoulder. I could still feel the kelp-bed tremors &
cold knuckles, the deep blue nomenclature & ringtone resurrecting a
phantom pain. And then I remembered that I always wanted to end a
poem with the word "polyurethane".

Duane Eddy Mows His Lawn

No difference between ocean & air here
"Voice of the Rolling Tide" as Mike says thinking of the
Gnostic Worm?

Open range cactus surf dramas
born of the sea & coastal fogs
a liquid territory landing with a THUD
as opposed to a SPLASH

outside the realm of these Byzantine street hassles

Dark pacific swamp mirrors shattered in the sun
a last breath, a tunnel of light, a trapdoor in the surf
spun from aluminum samples & a limited playlist

Their several garlands hoist ensigns of light & proportion
crashing like a scrap-iron accordion
into a pool of stained-glass violins

The Bride of Frankenfish

The shadows in this town are all wrong
    but what does that say about the light
stalling out in the heavy ocean haze?
        like me I guess another sea creature reciting
    the tide chart confessing to everything
                pure blue turquoise & slanted
    green sea beach pine logistics
as they pertain to the drum machine in the pavement
    set alongside the spaghetti western sky
    like the jewel of denial

True Romance

This seaweed tequila takes me back, I said.
I can taste the winter swell.

Sea-stone green. Dreamsicle orange.
A silver blanket of ocean mist.

The Garden of Earthly Delights like a bottomless
cup of coffee
looking for the pulse of Punta Baja.

I'd say keep your sunglasses on & lose the accent.

Tincture of opium is recommended, she said,
a Coleridge-in-Malta situation no doubt.

Back in the carbon era
she would have been named
Muriel Nitrate & the long paddle out a
true measure of desire.

Palisades

It feels like my brain has liquified & is sloshing up against the inside of my skull. People pay good money to feel like this & here I am getting it for free. This morning's all about the fog & thin drizzle, drin thizzle, damp & eternal-like. I can step between the rain drops if I shut my eyes & think about something else, but it's a long way from here to there, & I can't find my shoes.

Paint it Turquoise

The bare knuckles of the coast
at low tide
        Bluedark descending
    ghost riders in the sky
      above the Cowboy Surfshop
Today is somebody's birthday
       Nobody I know
She said her name was Frankie Johnnie
      I was sharing a smoke with Art Gomez
          pushing into the darkness
    fishtailed down dirt roads with Mexicans
    and their sisters
"You a surfer hey boy?"
      I was a boy then
         You couldn't break my heart
    I had poisoned myself deliberately
    Had visions, stood outside God's house
  in the rain
       He wasn't home
"Frankie Johnnie? What kind of name is that?"
"French" she said
      I would have thought Paris,
   Texas myself but then
  what do I know

Shell Game

for Noel Black

"I is another" Arthur Rimbaud.

"I yam what I yam" Popeye the Sailor Man.

Sean Penn reprising Jeff Spicoli but playing me,

"Aloha, Ezra Pound."

This song & dance is dedicated to
José Throwhammer, Jenny Staccato,
& Tina Damp (you know who you are)

Pale moon
fluttering in a corner of the sky
                            spilling salt-
        water
                        across the swamp known as Beach
Street
        the silver & the gold
                        & so forth
turquoise & chrome

                    — a vast expanse, a great expense —

    I'd trade in this sunburn for a sea-blue El Camino
    w/wings
                    but deals like that just don't happen anymore.

Strange bodies hovering outside the cheap cigarette store

        there has to be an explanation
                            & I'm working on it
        but it spooks the horses

Mullosks at the Gate

It's all about the way the tide rocks back
& the anchored wind
as sketched out
in an Arabic moonbook
stuttering like a No Vacancy sign
outsourced to
a ripple-thread of neon
E-changing above the swamp garden
just as my heart would if it had wings instead of aluminum siding
moist & trembling in the late afternoon
haze of smog lingering
& the palm trees they genuflect right there on the pavement

This is the season of uncontested mercy & acoustic glass
as it might be superimposed
beyond the genius of the sea
& you can really bite down into it when you're wrecked
on nickel shots & love & you've lived to tell lies about it

& so the sky tips down it seems only for you
seeing as your tattoo owes more to *Paradise Lost*
than to *The Upanishads*
dealt from your deck of wet petals

& soon the coast road is humming your tune
& I'm assuming a wall of mist like shattered chrome
drifts through your veins if there is such a place
just so we'll know when we get there

Invasion of the Body Surfers

Somehow we missed that
           radiant remnant of sky
        tucked like blue velvet over the palisades

but we've got the ocean to think about
        & an empty parking lot to hold hands with
           when we leap beneath the wave
lit with carbonated sunlight
      like beer bottles hurled against the crumbling sea wall

Your inexorable eyes
        bend no more than the cycloramic tide
obliquely sequined although I
           never thought its prophetic sequel would be
drenched in sunset
    lavished with impartial tears
        veering on azure blades above the splintered
paradigm its strings recast in silver

unlike the shadow painted on the sand
      already rusting in the salt mist that drops like a chunk of concrete

& I was wearing the commemorative t-shirt

        paddling back to the hard-luck land of turquoise
to look for you

Leaning into it

I took the easy way out
one step forward, three steps back.
My heart on a shelf in the discount aisle
the late afternoon wind
revising the weather map.

Changed the bandages in the rest
room of a Shell Station.
Kept my shades on in the Ebb Tide.
"Poured we libations unto each the dead."
A glass of beer & a shot of bourbon.
Blind graybeard black dude
Tiresias Theban.

The fading blue
sky my only reference point.
A Chevelle Super Sport burning oil
in the parking lot.

Eddie said "You should always take
four of anything." There were only three
to choose from—in the name of the father,
& of the son, & Zuma
Beach. I had a one-way ticket.

I liding my tattoos behind a forged
prescription at the pharmacy. It is
always summertime
somewhere.

Return of the Creature

AMAZING GRACE, WHERE IS THY STING
I wasn't talking to her
I was talking to the
avenging angel
tattooed on her ankle

STEEPED IN RUIN & CANDLELIGHT
I said I'd prefer a milkfed steel
tidewater canto
at sunset
& an unobstructed view

REALITY DISTORTION FIELD
It was more like snorting meth
w/Jacques Cousteau
than reciting *Sailing to Byzantium*
backwards

UNFINISHED BUSINESS
The Tibetan monk you resembled
in profile only
had a crowbar up his sleeve
which is just the thing when your
eyes snap like a rubber band
& the shadow of your heart
wrapped in tinfoil
discovers a new use for gravity

LOS LAVALAMPS
Reinventing the light as it would
seaward reflect
the walls of a tidepool clock

A BEND IN THE HAZE
Dreamed of Joanne & Donald
walking in Oaxaca
beneath a sky scorched by
turquoise flames

DARKER THAN YOU
The light is endless but it doesn't have anything
to do with us
wherever we walk
holding up our end of Eternity
"Not to be sold east of the San Andreas Fault"

AFTER THE GOLD RUSH
Walking back across the sand
leaving no footprints or trace
that I'd ever been there at all

HIGH SEAS DRIFTER
The moan of a rusted harmonica
bending palm trees in the fog

LONG TRIP OUT
You occupy a shadow
the rain gathering above the beach

That you were there at all
should have been enough

SULTANS OF SWING
Whatever drowned indulgence resigns
the threat of remembering
obvious intentions
the beach road humming like a wire
exhausted all lingering regret

I CAN ONLY RETURN TO THE
WAVY DEPTHS THAT I NEVER
LEFT IN THE FIRST PLACE
while those I used to know
            & whose company I carried
concede the rhyme
            in some other world
                        too far from mine
with words I might have heard
            some other time

Float Switch

Each wave's black as a field of dahlias

w/a wicked drop reflected

               back thru silver bells & whistles

        carved white marble inside

like dawn's early light

    echoing in an empty

        24 oz. Tecate can

            smeared with lipstick

Water & Power

Where was I then? What was I listening to? Oh, myself, no doubt, alone & humming a tune I can't remember. Did you say something? Of course you did. I understood every word I pretended to hear. Low end torque & rumble of mid-tide surf wrapping in around the point, foam washing up across the sand, late afternoon blue haze of sky gone gold around the edges. Your eyes were like damp footprints evaporating on the sidewalk & I was feeling like a flashlight on a moonless night the power gone & the rain sweeping in from the south.

Bring Me the Head of Eddie Vedder

I had loaned her my crown of thorns
& before she gave it back she had it
cleaned & sharpened for me

The wind raking the eucalyptus
blue turquoise green & tinsel
raw beach concrete

& the 36 chainsmoking buddhas in my hip pocket
were preaching a kind of punk compassion I
could really learn to dance to

Like a message in lipstick scrawled
onto a tidepool mirror
nobody knows what it means but
everyone understands it'll break if you
drop it which is what keeps us
coming back for more

The girl with the crucified seagull
tattooed on her back
said she knew something I didn't

She told me where it was but I had to find it myself

My skull packed with wet sand
pure as the driven foam

Shipped by Mule from Slovakia

Too late to change languages.

That look in your eye
never so near as when you're far away.

Something quieter, perhaps darker, turns inward
& dissolves in the pale light leaking from a sky of
tarnished silver.

But I can wait.

Sometimes the wind in the eucalyptus
is the way the dead talk to us.

Burnt orange & compensatory

She was standing naked at the window
next to a small Pembroke table
upon which sat my keys & my wallet & a candle
unlit
        because it was midday & the sun blasted intense
light down from a sky that was impossibly
high & blue
            & all I could see was her silhouette
as if cut from a book on the Black Arts
if you need me to say it
        sharing a seaweed cigarette there is
sand in the bed & beach tar on the soles of our feet
            music drifting in from the other room
Patti Smith or Mingus
           I couldn't say for sure
there were damp shadows in my ear
& the Coleridge I read that morning I found it to be
instructive
        like the punctuation marks I chose to ignore
in my copy of the *Tao Te Ching*
        which I forgot to mention was casually placed
on the table between my wallet & the candle "This is a
still life" she said & I thought yes, this is still
life
        or at the very least a 60/40 split

Welcome to Paradise

Between the pavement & the ocean sky
    just steps from where the coast
        road cuts its sectioned asphalt bleached
by the sun & fogs & vibroned tire treads
    of who knows how many cars and trucks
        careening into the mist
we parked & stumbled to find a steep
    crooked sandy trail
        down from panoramic cliffs

    intervals of rusty eucalyptus
        gargling the seabreeze
            like a flooded carburetor

        A neat pile of regurgitated fishbones
        in the center of the path
        like a nest of crystals in the sun

Another time I lost my sunglasses here

            inside mineshafts of raw pacific steel

    between the spanking cold & the damp

so that I had to blink to remember my name
& offshore breezes whispered so deciduously into the vast
unobserved platitude of ocean haze

something that was indicated or that could only be read upon the
rusted dashboard dials of a derelict Buick
rotting & sunken
decapitated in a ragged seaside vacant lot
adjacent to the tideflat
as in ancient crime scene photographs where detectives stand
& a uniformed patrolman points
the lurid implication of what lies hidden in the weeds

    but in the sand gravel parking lot
    where the pavement gleams wetly out of the past
        seems set like a jewel in the last stretch of land before
    the heaving Pacific
            swept in red sunset turquoise
    drizzled in the milk of alleyways purpled w/blood or mist
        swamped in a brown corner by Rembrandt
    with simple manifestations of allegorical contingencies
            trembling like a drop of dew in anticipation
    maybe Golgothas & la luz de Oriente
      flying in off the lip of the Pacific
    night & day crashing the sunburned sidewalk
    the sky rocking back on its heels

    between the dancer & the dance

    waiting for the tide to wrap in around the jetty

    drifting
              half your life at least
      the half you can still remember

& it was like silk or aluminum out there
at that depth & from the rolling surface tension lifted
shallow roses & a deeper gloom than all your Topangas
shrouded in smoke & mist of Aztec or
Abyssinian origin but with hula girls
tragic on a sand road in the lemon dusk
vacant & inexcusable except for the
way their hips move & the rustling of
grass skirts like the rainy cape of pneumatic
kelp groves rocking underwater to the
swoop & dazzle of ocean tides
& the bubbling under

Vapor Eyes

for Pamela

The ocean breeze
strumming the palm
trees makes a sound like a
hydraulic ukulele
played through a diesel engine
rumbling down a lonely stretch of the coast highway
on the next-to-last day of summer
& you're riding shotgun

or maybe it was me
getting all Proustian about bamboo windchimes
    & that wisp of cloud that followed us from Pismo
        like Blake's worm   hoisted from the wreckage
            of derivative sunlit streets near the beach

    just another notch in the pavement
    for the traditional Japanese mariachi punk band
    that sets the tempo here

"It's all about the music"
        even when it isn't
            although I'm not really listening
as the sun flares out into a feather of excess acetylene
& you do your little grind for me

With No Purpose Other
Than to Prevail

It was Tuesday
I had a Guinness for breakfast
& went surfing

my seaside algorithm got the best of me

so stoked later I bench-pressed a Cadillac
    singing baby please don't go
            back to the monster mask
            factory

The tamale lady was parked under a
blue sky that screamed for frijoles & rice
pico de gallo
    & all the leaky valve stems
    in the *Tao Te Ching*

        Sea Sea Rider
        in B-flat
        breaking left off the incoming ocean
        mist
                under the now pink
                blue gray orange & white sky
                tapping the prehistoric
                wah-wah pedal

Leucothea, Su Tung-p'o, & Percy Sledge vs Godzilla
bringing it all back home

Standing on the Nose
in a Stylish Manner

Know ye that on the right hand of the Indies
there is an island called California,
very near the terrestrial Paradise…

— Garci Rodríguez Ordóñez de Montalvo, circa 1510

Listening to the extended version of
I'll Be Your (Broken) Mirror
as palm trees tumble in the wind

    Streets tilting down
        towards the beach
    Candles flickering on
        Mexican voodoo shrines
           underwater

NORTH OF MALIBU
Ocean spills over edge of sky
all at once
in B-minor

. . . .

    Turkey buzzard gliding over the coast
    highway
        —quick moment—
    1. think of Lew Welch
    2. turn the corner

A future self revisiting a past self,
        that was me, once
paddling back & forth across the River Mitsuse

back & forth

in Japanese

Lovely *Doubloons* in the mail today
        poems by Sunnylyn, collages by Micah
        Mardi Gras 2011

. . . .

        BALBOA, BIG SUR, BOLINAS
        bubbles
                rattling
                        far out at sea

WHISPERED IN THE RATTLING PALM LEAVES
LIKE A HAIKU WITH A HACKSAW IN IT
The sky wasn't the color of your eyes
although it blinked & turned away as you do
when I'm being stupid

PHILOSOPHICAL INVESTIGATIONS, INC.
Too many levels of reality to scroll through
never enough
                but then God
(a known alcoholic with a criminal record
& a pink hat)
                was nowhere to be found

I tossed the *I Ching* every day for 20 years
as if that might clear the clutter of choices
made & not made
        & even when the coins came up snake eyes
I still paddled out in my
        catholic boy wetsuit

to charge one last mushy beach break
before the sun set
& the world & you
plunged
into darkness

———————————————————

Other times, other places
memories, feelings
too heavy to be lifted

———————————————————

I knew those mirrors needed proof
beyond the bend of the tide
if only to reinvent the central nervous system
in the dyslexic translation
from neon to concrete

All my life I danced it that way
the loop, the wedge, the hook
one foot in a watery grave & the other
on the edge of something really vast
like a vast undiscovered continent that
disappeared
long before I was born

& although I have no idea what time it is
late & early
the mermaid with the sea-mist tattoo
gathers kelp blossoms
somewhere beyond the reef

where I would love to take you some day
but there has to be a reason
Each stares down through the other
looking for a way back

World Domination On $3 A Day

The morning bends upon the
song of a redwing blackbird
across the busted up alley that drops
down to the beach

You need not fear the Eskimos
drinking Vietnamese coffee
nor the waterlogged legions
of the dead leaving their damp
footprints on the concrete
indelible
like the Roman alphabet

The waves gargle a rainy esperanto

Except for the noise the beach is quiet

You do not understand

The heart of the sea is silence

On the Eve of the Year
of the Green Wood Horse

Several possibilities come to mind. Tack them to the Mexican voodoo shrine. The Year of the Black Tar Horse, for example. But the blue agave sky, no one voice can encompass or describe. The rapid lid of the tide extends the thunder of hooves later translated by eucalyptus leaves & shipped by mule to 1211 Venice Blvd. Estimated delivery date February 4, 1956.

There was the bottle of tequila, not half empty nor half full, just half there, like the rest of us. The light was golden & you could fold it up & take it with you when it was time to go. Broken sea shells, yellow weeds, the rattling dead thistle. Sun-dazzle. The seething tide / wave-break foam. Proteus to Kanaloa.

The horse might have been an appaloosa but it was hard to tell because we were looking into the sun. Several possibilities come to mind. You leave them on the sand for someone else to find. Your heart is a framed portrait of the wind riding in on a southwest swell, I said, & your eyes are windows left open in the rain.

Love could be another way to say it

Past Ruin'd Ilion
The early morning light igniting the lip of the wave
the color of mermaids
    as in the fresco
        spray-painted on the seawall
only half-remembered

Thou restless, ungathered
She leaned against me
the way the fog
leans along the shore

Hermosa Beach Blues
Spring......
Too long......
Godzilla......

Seahorses

A powder of yellow-tinged light dusted her cheek. A breath could blow it all away. I sat outside the vintage Boulderado Airstream with my unforgiven friends. Few in number but great in alcohol consumption. Fighting the overwhelming fatigue. Ming Fatigue. Flailing at quatrains. Beguiling the mile high verisimilitude. Thin air.

Micah with his slow eye predetermined, Dunagan passed out on the lawn with his shirt off, the patient crystal circumspection of Sunnylyn, & Miguel, the shepherd, fending off immortality behind a pair of dark glasses he stole from Beyoncé. I was only barely there, had to check every now & again to see if I was still casting a shadow, however pale, to reassure myself that the cerveza had a place to go, to swirl & bubble down as though to quench a thirst, itself a lost cause.

"The eternal fellowship that swept unseen, flitting, fleet, against the stagelit Airstream deck, elicits tears in retrospect" (as I wrote in a dark moment lifted briefly from sleep & forgotten). Thus in the plastic orange radiance of twin cartoon seahorse barlights afixed to the silver armament of the Airstream International did I rally in my own recitation of memorized poems from those long passed from us, if only to preempt the neglect a heart seeks & hides, that deeper respect so tied to strains of a continuous music. Long before, long after. As I thought the sublime distraction worth articulating or why push on. The mere pursuit or intent itself held us in its sway.

Drawn Blank

for Pope Benedict XI & Bill Berkson

A seagull wheels & pivots in the sky
describing the arc of a compass

a prayer-wheel windchime
racking up the zeroes

a roundelay

a self-devouring hula hoop
                    rolling downhill

I don't know, Bill, what else?

                    a bubble in a mile of milk?

something concentric like Kandinsky
singing
                    doo-wah-ditty-dum
                    ditty-doom

& standing outside the Del Taco in Ventura
on Chinese New Year
                                        in the rain
              Giotto dips his brush in red
              paint
                              & in one continuous stroke
                    draws a perfect circle

Hart Crane Sleeps with the Fishes

Not the Dark Rose but the CHRYSANTHEMUM

sea anemone

an illustration from The Western Book of the Dead

You ask me who do I consider to be the greatest surrealist of all time
& I say Busby Berkeley

Surrender the spilled drink

put a fork in it

The earliest maps show California as an island

Hazy blue afternoon laying flat on its back
beach pavement running all the way to Yokohama beneath the
variable shade of windswept cypress & tortured rhododendron

On ancient maps sea monsters represent the Great Unknown

"The most fearful of monsters is a well-known friend
slightly altered" (Kobo Abe)

sashimi tacos, two for 5 bucks

Not the fortune palms but the eucalyptus grove slope
just before it rains

& not the Garden of the Hesperides but Zuma Beach
when the seaweed is in bloom

The Shining
for Alan Opstedal

Something glitters in the sand
tiny mirrors, grains of glass, dust of
stars or the sun-
light all broken up on the rippling
ocean out there
next to I don't know diamonds
chrome
capsules of mercury
el coronado
(sparkle, like the story my brother
tells about being jumped by a gang one night
outside the Venice High gym
they wanted money but
he didn't have any money so one of them
yanked off the St. Christopher medal he wore around
his neck— Why do you think they did that?
I asked him & he said, Because it was
s h i n y

Mark It Zero

Did the tribal stomp & shuffle on the bluff
above the beach as the swell rolled in

heavy green water cut with foam

Dromedary days on the drought-stricken
central coast only make me thirsty

Hummingbird interrogates the red flowering aloe

Is there an answer for everything?

I didn't think so

Sand in the Grooves

It Feels Like Nowhere
A northwest swell brings waist to head high surf
during the more favorable tides
then the wind shifts & the mind goes blank
like a black tar reckoning on the pier at high noon

Going Coastal
The ocean breeze competing w/the
traffic on Hwy 1 for our
eternally divided attention
as we race down the eucalyptus alleyway
into the neon eyes of the sea

27 Shades of Kool-Aid
I often think silver & steel, chrome & velvet, the
vaulted cathedral architecture beneath the pier
at half past sunset as the fog steps down

Sunlight spinning like a quarter on the sidewalk
It was summertime & nothing was easy
except you & the Tibetan Book of the Dead way you
parted your hair

How the Mayans
Invented Television

We can look up into the clear
sky   it's pearl-colored though not as
mysterious as it should be
this time of day

    The wandering streets
    seem somehow lighter than the
        concrete and asphalt they're made of
    & there should be a wind but
            there isn't
      as the setting sun goes to work on you
           with a samurai sword & a road flare

The foam that washes across the sand is
lit from the inside   just like you
    maintaining radio silence
      like fainting Desdemona of the Andes
        wading through the seaweed
reciting all the tide tables from Genesis
to Revelations
      & every blood type from rose to rust
as my brain caves in to Hawaiian music
      & maybe the mist parts like a beaded curtain
   & nothing is revealed

The B-side of a once
& future flashback

The dark side of her eyes
crease the sunset
        as you would the petals of some
                tropical flower

maybe a rare orchid
        with blooms the color of burnt steel

& that she proves Zeno's law with every step she takes
the highway disappearing over her shoulder
like smoke

        I told her I could drive the PCH forever

just that stretch from Point Mugu to Santa Monica
& back again

        A region of rare power & inspiration
tapping the source of dreams lost & dreams
that have yet to be dreamt
            like hillsides & bluffs
                crumbling into the sea
(coastal erosion
is a state of mind)

        "The world is ruled by letting things take their course.
        It cannot be ruled by interfering.
        If you try to change it you will ruin it.
        If you try to hold it you will lose it." (*Tao Te Ching*)

All that cement will turn to sand eventually

Be patient

————————————————————————————————————

Night sifting down thru the smog

there wasn't anything we could do about it

The streets with their shadows tucked neatly into place

I wondered at the genius of it—

She never said a word
she didn't have to

The streets were hers
& the shadows
& the night

Spanish Word

It's mid-morning between tides
& my heart's another nickel in the
jukebox. I'd like to break off a corner
of it on that mushy left dropping in on
the lip of bowl. That kind of passion digs
in on the dark side of bliss like an aquasonic
boom rattling the cathedral glass that lines the
tide pools just north of here. I felt like I was
embalmed in the ocean haze. A bar of
tombstone wax turning into candlelight
in my pocket. My resumé fit nicely onto a
grain of sand. A grain of sand the size of your fist.
Your left fist which is roughly the same size as
your heart.

Find Me a Golden Street

Nothing really belongs to us. We can't afford the clutter. If only time lags a bit between X and infinity w/late night street traffic a distant pulse. In this zone we are given formulas to sustain crime & divinity. Why not the tropic denial? A game of Chinese whispers. Streets dark w/ragged palm trees truncated by the fog, lopped off telephone poles, invisible high-tension wires. I was raised in this marooned city, the glow of a lava lamp behind smoked glass framed by Spanish tiles & stucco. Corinthian columns by way of Tijuana. Any given moment doctored the script. Beach town neon pharmacy parking lot. Felt the heat of the midnight pavement radiate up thru the soles of my sneakers. This must be the fourth corner, the one the earth turns upon. It doesn't belong to us. My ankles are sore. Light played on the surface of the stagnant brown sludge of the canals. That was a memory. It's all different now. Sherman Canal where I smoked hashish w/a girl who had a broken nose. The sidewalk stained with rust, or blood. Money would change that. Them. The sea breeze stalled out at the intersection of Venice & Lincoln Blvd so that I could cross the street without looking. Heard the wave's message whispered in a bottle at 3am the door latch broken & the still night air eaten up by a candle flame. Incense. No where to take it finally. We never owned any of it. The tide shifted. It was too subtle for anyone to notice. No apologies, I remember now, everything has been forgotten. We never asked forgiveness. Slight bend in the streetlights. Sand in your clothes. Drive by in an old beat-up Pontiac looking over yr shoulder. I still consider this place to be home, although it no longer exists. The sound of waves reclaim the distance I have traveled since.

Stirring up the shadows

1. Turn on the TV

2. Don't watch it

3. Remember taking peyote in 1976?

4. Water on the brain

5. ...uh...

6. Philip Guston

7. *Paradise Lost* vs the later *Maximus Poems?*

8. Spiderwebs in the wind

9. A combination of small south & northwest groundswells delivering waves of up to five feet at north-facing beaches as I gather a bouquet of broken glass & rusty windchimes for the French girl with leukemia who at this very moment is gently knocking at my door

All Debts Real & Imagined

He had dreams which he used like a chainsaw
& a wife that was leaning the other way
                        purple thistles / broken bottles
        "gracefully relinquished"
Black branches scratching the clouds
onshore winds
                        Pakistani glasspacks rumbling in the night
& you find yourself
upsidedown beneath a porticoed heaven
                        beating on an iron skillet

        Ruin hath taught me thus
                        out on the tideflats
                (not infinite but eternal?)

Shades of blue in the haze

                adorned or should I say wounded with
                pale light

The truth is just as elusive

                        on a windy day the
                        seagulls get blown off course
                        just like me

electricity konks out

hidden details / clouds in the sky

Bikini Doll w/her mood enhancing indulgences
& x'd-out eyes blue under sedation
more or less diaphanous
staggers in amongst these universal concepts

like trying to parallel park the Theory of Relativity

Just because I lived that then
why should anyone know or care

(if the truth be told)

contrary to popular belief

we was nowhere

A surfboard in every refrigerator

Some late & early morning
fog on stilts
  The backstage pinwheel orchestra
    pounding out the 445th chorus
  of *Heartbreaker*
& if you consider how life here has
  become like a polished chrome
quaalude at the
    bottom of a motel swimming pool
  then you'd hike your skirt up for me
      when the sun drops like a shot bird
  pulling the mist over your eyes
  dark like silver & damp
    inside a delicate architecture comprised of
fishbones & concrete
    & silk things that rust at the edges of tide pools

& I'm smacking my lips at every pantomime shimmer
    that ripples on the surface of your tender denial
which is why I'm loading the squirt gun with tequila
& rocking the mortuary RayBans
at midnight
    with knocks & pings in the terza rima
like bells ringing
underwater

  TEN THINGS I DO UNDERWATER

Fall thru the mirror
slick back my eyes
listen to the *Songs of the Whales*
on headphones
watch late night reruns of Lloyd Bridges in *Sea Hunt*
nod out
wonder what happened to all of my *Sub-Mariner* comic books
count the bubbles
roll the dice
breathe

You Don't Know What Love Is

I had cut the deck to the Ace of Tentacles. Don't look back they say but we always do. The road to Playa de las Palmas was arduous. I was riding the clutch & she was commenting on the tuck-and-roll upholstery. There are things that are meant to be whispered like seafoam across the sand & I told her so. We had been running on fumes ever since we crossed the border & we'd gone too far to turn back now. It's late at night & it starts to rain. Windshield wipers slapping like a metronome keeping time. It's difficult to see in the blinding glare of oncoming headlights, but is that Janet Leigh hurtling through space towards the Bates Motel?

To Our Lady of Wet Sand
as she swims down from the parking
lot naked beneath her tattoos & silver

Martian blue eyes
hypnotized by the sea
I guess beauty can only
cop a plea as the sky bleeds
like a jelly doughnut
& my sunglasses don't
hide a thing

The Heart Sutra
inscribed on a grain of sand
reminds me of sipping a Primo
while listening to reggae music
in the Aloha Island Grille
on a dark night in February
with water in my ear

I may have looked like the
shroud of Turin but I felt just like
King Kong on a bender
teaching the nuns how to
cheat at liar's dice
& bragging about surfing Todos Santos
w/a girl in my fist

February 34th

Bowing deeply in the 4 directions
up, down, forward, & back
as aforesaid by Circe

"You have the right to remain unconscious" etc.
say the angels who crown me w/such
pleasant poppies

& filling the squirt gun with blanks
the day gets away from me like a fast horse

It starts to rain, I'm out of cigarettes, the
toilet works but you have to jiggle the handle
when you flush it

"Shall two know the same in their knowing?"
probably not

Against expectation I've got the feeling that
I'm beginning to look like the perfect stranger
ordering a Monster Taco at the drive-up window
of the Karma Repair Shop

Way Down Below

If you asked me for a smoke & I bloodied yr nose
my bones would still ache w/longing
& my dreams like the wraparound wind
would lull you sleep as I unlace my sneakers
& cradle you like a fever

Selling Books for Drugs

The octopus has eight arms
three hearts
& an internal combustion engine
but if you look behind the
beach tar mascara
you'll find eyes that exhibit the same
variable high cloudiness that
defines the sky this time of day
reinventing the concrete
drizzled in pale light
hypnotizing seagulls
& even with the surf feathering out
& engines idling in the cypress
variegated syllables of sand & foam
reclaim the streets
& whatever is buried beneath the
kelp grove is going to have to stay there
& speaking of sea monsters
how is it that I find myself lurking
in the wavy depths of your eyes
when I should be breathing fire & devouring
whole sections of the coast highway
as palm trees rattle & sway
like love at first sight

Primer Gray Tikis in the Mist

for Dale Herd

An ill-advised leap from the pier
because Jim Castro said I didn't have the balls

I had the balls all right but not the
brains to tell him to go fuck himself

What was it 1972?

       Way out at the far end of space & timelessness
       like it was only yesterday, or the day before that

Are these the same blue eyes that learned to
read the tide that year at Playa del Rey?

Probably not   given what we is now

       Anyway it was really Dockweiler Beach
the sewage effluent & the El Segundo refinery
made it a "special" place

     I never knew it any different
       my DNA all over that scene

I should have died in TJ that time
I had my ticket punched & everything

shuffling through the damp pages of every ocean

in the backseat at 90 miles an hour

& she was gazing out thru the windshield

        inventing thermodynamics

    pictured as a beautiful blue tide

        rushing in beneath the burnt-pink windows

of no place special

like what's left when you drain the pool

& I never noticed until someone mentioned

there was blood all down the side of my face

Rust never sleeps

Numb w/the relentless details
you could bounce a quarter off the sky
or break an eyeball in a Mexican stand-off
w/the Three Graces
which is reason enough to invoke
Tethys, Amphitrite, Kalypso,
& various lesser sea nymphs & mermaids
cascading vertically on the steps
of an extended vacation
sharpening a southern accent w/a book of Latin
verses & a coping saw
mumbling like no one I know
on a streetcorner in Venice Beach near Sherman Canal
saying "The Egytians built the world's first
canal almost 4 thousand years ago"
a fact that inspires visions of the pharaohs carrying shovels
& walking sideways
& who knows what desire sleazing up w/the late
afternoon breeze stirring the dust in yr brain
like a black pajama death wish shuffling through beach sand
which could be a
heroic tragic flaw if you've got the lungs for it
but with pinpoint hollow eyes reading Ecclesiastes
thru binoculars
in the grip of your own personal endless summer
with all expenses paid
except one

On the Use of Symbolism in
18th Century French Romantic Poetry

Whistling past the wrecking yard
watching the sun rise through
a beaded curtain

WAVE PATTERN CARVED IN STONE

septic shock

Spilling coffee on my way
back following the damp foot-
prints of some sea nymph or dakini

"She who walks in the sky"

Assuming you recognized her
from the centerfold in the
King James Bible
which is about as close
as you're likely to get

The seagreen lipstick a dead giveaway
not to mention the porcelain eyes

Whether you fell or were pushed it's
the same difference

The first law of gravity is
heavier than the 2nd
—is there a 3rd?

She was a day crossed off the Mayan calendar
& I was staggering across the wet sand
shedding fish scales that
glittered like silver coins in the mist

Considering the Heart
as a Flotation Device
for Joanne Elizabeth Kyger

Dragonfly pauses to rest a moment on a strand of barbed wire

    its iridescent green & blue body
    its double set of transparent wings

        Bright cold winter sunlight is also blue

            Mississippi Half-Step Uptown Toodeloo

The undulating gaze
when the smoke clears & you have been
absolved in the crumbling light moist with tears that are neither yours
nor mine
        just gleamingly wet
                while the drama waits
somewhere
        w/a short list of places to go
                things to do
but it's all up to you

& the torch aloe (*arborescenes*) is just about ready to bloom

Valvoline

Some say one last kiss could have
made all the difference

    but the wet sand isn't talking & the wind
        cuts down the alley like Odysseus
            crossing off eternity on a pocket calendar

& no I don't believe we breathe the same air

2.
SUNSET AT TIERRA DEL FUEGO
A solo for steam-driven guitar

3.
    The light returning
    e quel remir
                suffused in haze
    silver in shadow
        la luz de Oriente
            in a sharkskin bikini

Guided by Voices

Early morning mid-tide pebbled glass

a kind of call & response scenario
& who isn't when you're
trying so hard to lose your balance

strumming the sand
The Needle in the Groove
& eucalyptus gargling the seabreeze

I'll let you do the math

There are perhaps other
more expedient methodologies
if you can but I never could

& worth its weight in greasy blonde platitudes
making the pavement sing

Long Story Short

A lovely accident waiting to happen
meets the scenic cruise we never shared

    & just as I assume that God must
        always carry a dictionary
            a little misdirection can go a long way

To learn why the gulls prefer one side of the
beach to the other requires the application of
geometric logic & prophetic dreams

        It seems I was reading *Meister Eckhart*
        thru the wrong end of a telescope

            missing a step while trying to cut my losses

                which is something that is better left to
                rust in the Elkhorn Slough
                    beneath a broken seashell

Sunlight streams in thru the cypress
& when the road bends so do you

The Wrong Goodbye

Fire-breathing dragons, leviathans & Godzillas
emerging from the deep
     along w/something that resembles an
                         octopus in a leotard?

The setting sun burns a hole in the dark silk sky

     a wall of fog drifting in off the water...

          you thought it looked like Frida Kahlo descending a staircase
               I thought it looked more like Percy Sledge in a limousine

The cypress sighs
          a breezy whistle
                    shadows on pebbled glass

The steep fogmist gave me yet another reason
to double back thru the cuts

               Ape in the rain at Cuernavaca
                         versus dice games on the ocean floor

There's no equivalent & no disclaimer

silk & neoprene
                         variations on a theme

from one slippery mind to another

Hula Doll in a Helium Hat

It all happens somewhere beyond the
post-apocalyptic dog & pony show
dreamed in another language I can't translate
scrawled across the narrow sky

    bending sunlight on a
    flat empty beach no where to hide
        waves flashing silver blue
            translucent eucalyptus bulldozer

This place you now inhabit
hit with brushed chrome & darkened mirrors that
deny your reflection as you might gaze out through
windows painted black

    it is the flawed pearl you've learned to treasure

& just as the tides answer to a mythology
older than the gravity that sleeps in every
stone cobbled along the shore

Elvis hath left the building

Travels in Abyssinia,
the Harar & Santa Cruz

It's dark down here on the sand
although the sky's lit up like
Mega-Millions gnawing on a lightbulb
above the pearl-handled tide

& the way your breathing sort of
ripples thru the mist
makes me want to pull the shade on
a thousand years worth of
ocean sunsets

but I'm hooked on whatever happens after
as the streets give up their
trembling denial
& the moon hauls out it's
black velvet paintings
each worth at least a half-
minute of silence

pacific standard time

. . . .

> *Vista Point*
> Ornamental pavilions of rust
> consecrate the shoreline
> caught in the glare of fishscale chrome
> as far as the eye can see

. . . .

We get that golden aura off the
late afternoon sun & we're several bottles past
the trembling blue agave light

as at Playa San Pedrito
previously breathing fire & sea-mist
The initials carved there in the half-light
explaining nothing as I can only remember
the taste of her lips
& the smooth transition

. . . .

Angle of Repose
Bending in the rain
    like a double-jointed palm tree
as the flashlight batteries give out...

    Arcades of black eternity in blue mascara
        out there in the windblown seaweed
the meaning of time like a stolen wristwatch
& you can sing along if you want to
following these damp footprints back to when you
never knew the difference

. . . .

    When asked of their origins
    the Chumash point to the west
    out over the Pacific Ocean
    as being the home of the First People
    a place they call the Land of the Dead
    where the Great Spirit lives
    in a crystal cave
    on the bottom of the sea

. . . .

BROKEN SILVERGREEN SENTENCES
SUSTAINED BY THE LYRIC INSTABILITY
OF WET STONES BLINKING IN THE FOAM
She was stapled like a cloud
to a corner of the sky

the color of beach pavement
  & I was a wine-stained tombstone cutback
as ominous as a shadow
   falling across a bead curtain
    in another room

The sunset glass made it a perfect setting for
a soul session with the drainpipe crew
& we danced on the string of a tropical memory
    as she always preferred something euphoric
a tidepool with a fuse in it
for example
    lit & sputtering
as long as it left a scar

. . . .

  The water was cold
    the waves had a glassed-in purity
  that shattered into white foam
     with plumes of mist flying back
   (the dragon in the waves)

. . . .

Circling the Drain
  like trance music & sun stroke
to float the memory
   sleazy but essential

  & no more shipwrecked kimonos
to worship in silhouette
    where we're the only survivors left
  to blink in the fog
    & wonder why

Acknowledgments

Some of the poems herein were previously published (sometimes in different shape & form) in the following books and chapbooks: *Kamikaze Blvd* (Sudden Press, Half Moon Bay, CA, 1985), Jungles (Gas Editions, 1992), *Sand in the Vaseline* (Mike & Dale's, San Francisco, CA, 1997), *Like Rain* (Angry Dog, San Francisco, CA 1999), *Crush* (surfZombie, Santa Cruz, CA, 2000), *The Road to Hollywood is Paved with Tacks & Suicide* (w/Michael Price, surfZombie, 2000), *Beach Blanket Massacre* (Smog Eyes, Playa del Rey, CA, 2001), *Next to Dreaming, or The Phone Never Rang* (Angry Dog/Midget Editions, 2002), *9th & Ocean* (Auguste Press, San Francisco, CA, 2002), *Variable High Cloudiness* (The Dozens, Santa Ynez, CA, 2002), *Nine Palms* (Aurthur Klang & Sons, Boulder, CO, 2002), *Radio Beach* (Pelican Press, San Mateo, CA, 2003), *Heavy Water* (w/Pamela Dewey, surfZombie, 2003), *Straight Up & Down* (Blue Press, Santa Cruz, CA, 2004), *The Deep End* (Plywood Press, 2004), *El Tsunami* (Auguste Press, San Francisco, CA, 2004), *Coastal Disturbance (Bikini Machine)* (Pale Music Press, Goleta, CA, 2005), *400 Hawaiian Shirts* (Detour Press, 2005), *Minus Tide* (Smog Eyes, Playa del Rey, CA, 2005), *Double Impact* (w/Michael Price, Blue Press, 2005), *On the Low* (Gallery Editions, Monterey, CA, 2006), Rare Surf, Vol. 2: New & Used Poems (Smog Eyes, Playa del Rey, CA, 2006), *Baja* (w/Pamela Dewey, Blue Press, 2006), *User's Manual to the Pacific Coast Highway* (Seven Fingers, Boulder, CO, 2007), *Saltwater Credentials* (w/Pamela Dewey, Blue Press, 2007), *Santa Cruz* (Blue Press, Santa Cruz, CA, 2008), *Maybe Ocean Street* (Airstream Editions, Boulder CO, 2009), *Deja Voodoo* (Blue Press, Santa Cruz, CA, 2010), *Drainpipe Sessions* (Otoliths, Australia, 2011), *California Redemption Value* (University of New Orleans Press, 2011), *Memory Foam* (Seven Fingers, 2013), *The Poetikal Works of Dude the Obscure* (Seven Fingers, 2014), *Curse of the Surf Zombie* (Smog Eyes, 2015).

Other poems have also appeared in a wide variety of magazines, newspapers, & online publications including *Mike & Dale's Younger Poets, Log, Gas, Blue Book, Big Bridge, Jack, Rolling Stock, Exquisite Corpse, Augustus Truhn's Magazine, Blind Date, Otoliths, Good Times Weekly, Prosodia, Creative Nonfiction, Yolanda Pipeline's Magazine,*

Night Palace, Frequency Audio Journal, Little Horse's Magazine. Please forgive me if I have forgotten any. Due to the passage of time & a rather scattered existence things get lost.

I thank the friends and editors who have taken the time and trouble to publish my works, in particular Noel Black, Micah Ballard, Sunnylyn Thibodeaux, and Michael Price.

Gratitude to poet Edward Ainsworth whose careful reading of the working manuscript of this book was heroic.

I must also thank poets Bill Berkson, Donald Guravich, Joanne Kyger, Lewis MacAdams, and Duncan McNaughton for their continued support and friendship.

The present volume would not have happened had it not been for the encouragement, sponsorship, and persistence of Noel Black and Julien Poirier. Gentlemen, I am in your debt.